STO

ACPL ITEM
3 1833 00300 3321
DISCARDED

1475d

D1616432

12-10-75

Smith
Ricardo
Marx

Claudio Napoleoni:

Smith
Ricardo
Marx

Translated by J. M. A. Gee

A Halsted Press Book
JOHN WILEY & SONS New York

© *in this translation*
Basil Blackwell 1975

All rights reserved. No part of this
publication may be reproduced, stored in
a retrieval system, or transmitted, in any
form or by any means, electronic,
mechanical, photocopying, recording or
otherwise, without the prior permission
of the publishers.

Translated by arrangement from Smith Ricardo Marx
Second Italian edition copyright © *1973*
Editore Boringhieri, Turin

Published in the USA by Halsted Press,
a division of John Wiley & Sons Inc., New York

Library of Congress Cataloging in Publication Data

Napoleoni, Claudio.
    Smith, Ricardo, Marx.

    Bibliography: p.
    Includes index.
        1. Economics—History   2. Marxian economics.
I. Title.
HB97.5.N3413   330.1   75–15962
    ISBN 0–470–63011–6

Printed in Great Britain

1888350

Contents

Foreword *vii*

Chapters

One: *The Present State of Economic Thought* *1*
Two: *The Physiocrats* *9*
Three: *Adam Smith* *25*
Four: *David Ricardo* *61*
Five: *Abstract Labour, Exchange and Capital in Marx* *99*

Readings

One: *Two Writings by François Quesnay* *115*
Two: *The 'Glasgow Lectures' of Adam Smith* *136*
Three: *Two Writings by David Ricardo* *153*

Index *193*

Foreword

In *Smith Ricardo Marx* Claudio Napoleoni has traced the development of several key themes in the history of economic thought, from the Physiocrats to Karl Marx. In the course of doing so, he has demonstrated how changing economic and social conditions have provoked an intellectual and philosophical reaction, as men have attempted to understand the nature of a new environment which they themselves have created. The spread of 'capitalism' necessarily transformed social and economic theory, and Napoleoni illuminates the nature of this transformation through his discussion and analysis of the development, in particular, of value theory and the theory of the so-called surplus or net product.

Though critical of Marx, Napoleoni's discussion of the writers concerned employs, in the main, a Marxist analytic framework of reference. As a result the book is given a coherence and unity which would otherwise have been difficult to achieve, and the interested student is presented with a stimulating interpretation of the development of ideas. Napoleoni presents a useful collection of original writings by François Quesnay, Adam Smith and David Ricardo at the end of the book.

I am grateful to Mr. Maurice Greig and Mr. E. H. Thompson for their help with the translation, and to Dr. E. M. O'Sharkey for translating François Quesnay's *Reply to M.H. etc*. I also thank Professor R. L. Meek for his kind permission to reproduce Quesnay's *Maxims* as translated in his *Economics of Physiocracy* (1963).

J. M. A. GEE   Dundee

One:

The Present State of Economic Thought

Ever since Marx's contribution, economic thought has been characterized by its division into two camps, one 'bourgeois' and the other Marxist. The essential difference between the two camps is that bourgeois economics does not place capitalism within an historical context, while Marxism regards capitalism as an historically defined reality. I must emphasize that this situation has lasted for more than a century and cannot simply be regarded as a feature of present-day thought. On the contrary, the situation is underlined by the fact that (1) bourgeois thought is deeply divided internally, (2) Marxist thought faces a number of problems which have become increasingly obvious.

I will attempt here to give a brief summary of the principal features of this situation; but I must stress that because of the necessarily schematic nature of the discussion I am obliged to exclude certain aspects entirely, and the discussion will be presented as a series of propositions, without any attempt at rigorous proof. In fact what follows is an outline guide rather than a systematic treatment.

We will begin by considering the characteristics of bourgeois economic thought. To understand its present 'crisis state' one needs to compare it with the bourgeois economic thought that held sway from the final decades of the nineteenth century to the economic crisis of 1929. During this period non-Marxist political economy was a unified body of science, internally consistent, which purported to give a rigorous analysis of the economic 'mechanism'.

At that time neo-classical theory, or marginalism, was based on the following three propositions.

(1) 'Modern' society is not divided into classes. It is true that there are different ways of participating in the productive or economic process—each individual has a different contribution to make, whether it be labour, natural resources, or capital. But there is no difference between individuals in so far as their position towards economic activity is concerned, since each one, like the next, is a supplier of some productive service.

(2) The social product is sub-divided between the suppliers of productive services according to naturally determined, objective laws, summed up by the expression 'marginal productivity theory' which relates the share of the social product to the productive services rendered by each supplier.

(3) The distributed product is made up of 'utilities' which can be compared and measured against each other and distributed accordingly. This implies that such utilities can be converted into values—and that value is a natural phenomenon because it is nothing other than the quantification of the social product's natural property of utility—that is, of its ability to satisfy needs.

Such, then, was the theoretical framework which suffered crisis at a particular time in the history of economic thought. The objective reasons why bourgeois economic thought entered into a crisis situation have to do with the economic and social history of capitalism; and there are also formal reasons, pertaining to the logic and internal coherence of marginal productivity theory.

The 'objective' factors may be considered in the following way. Marginal theory pictures an harmonious world, which tends towards 'static' or 'dynamic' equilibrium. Such a world can be described by reference to equilibrium positions and to economic processes which take place when there is an accidental departure from equilibrium, using models not dissimilar to those which natural science employs in describing the physical world. However, history has increasingly shown that capitalism is disharmonious and carries on rather by means of disequilibrium, crisis, and conflict. Bourgeois thought itself has recognized these various disequilibria, which may be regarded in outline terms as follows. First, there are overproduction crises which culminated in the slump that began in 1929. In the second place there are disequilibria in the level of development as between different parts of the world economy (the 'scandal of underdevelopment'). Third, capitalism exhibits un-balanced consumption, in the sense that despite the rapid growth of material wealth, some basic needs remain unsatisfied and, paradoxically, such needs are in general satisfied to a lesser and lesser degree. Finally, capitalism involves the destruction of natural resources and of the natural environment. More important than all these factors, however, is the existence within capitalism of a basic contradiction which, despite its great importance in the capitalistic order, bourgeois thought finds it difficult to recognize. This contra-diction consists of a systematic and inevitable conflict between the producers and the social relationship in which the producers find themselves. In other words, workers' opposition is the most un-compromising systematic disharmony within the system.

But, as I have said, there exist formal as well as objective reasons for the crisis in bourgeois economic thought. It is more difficult to deal with them in a schematic approach such as this, and I will limit myself to an account of the basic point at issue. Marginal theory falls into a contradiction when, according to its general assumptions, it attempts to formulate the concept of capital. On the one hand capital, in so far as it is a given original factor, is conceived—like labour—as one of the material prerequisites for the creation of wealth and hence of value; on the other hand capital, unlike labour, is presented as a value in itself—which supposes wealth already to exist. This difficulty appears in marginal theory in a variety of different ways, without changing its underlying nature.

One must not think, however, that bourgeois economic thought made no attempt to respond to its crisis state. Attempts have been and are being made with respect to both the objective and formal aspects of the crisis.

So far as the objective factors are concerned, state intervention has been called for under at least three headings: demand-regula-tion in order to cure overproduction; the control of distribution according to what may be called 'incomes policy'; and the pro-gramming of the production and consumption process.

Before seeing whether or not state intervention has been effica-cious we should show the particular way in which bourgeois thought, when calling for state intervention, is being at least in part inconsistent in the light of some of its basic assumptions. For, not only is state intervention outside the traditional liberal framework, but it also implies the negation of the fundamental concept of capitalism as a non-historic phenomenon. We shall see why this is the case for each of the interventions mentioned.

Demand-regulation through political economy presupposes that the market does not use some part of the savings that would be made under conditions of full utilization of productive capacity. But, if savings are useless or even harmful under so-called Keynesian conditions, then interest cannot be regarded as a reward which is necessary to the production process. Interest instead takes on the nature of a rent, which is how Keynes in fact saw it. Thus, the characteristic capitalistic income is reduced in status to an income typifying a precapitalistic economy.

Secondly, if one admits that the distribution of income must be regulated by a specific act of state it follows that distribution does not take place according to a natural mechanism. (It is as well to note the absurdity of presenting incomes policy as a way of restoring an objective mechanism. The 'labour productivity' to which incomes policy refers has nothing whatsoever in common with the 'marginal labour productivity' or neo-classical theory. Thus to say that wages must increase with 'labour productivity' is the same as saying that the rate of profit, which comes to be regarded as given, must remain unchanged.)

Thirdly, if consumption and production are controlled or programmed by the state, the 'consumers sovereignty' thesis is falsified, as is the thesis that the capitalist utilizes resources rationally.

In conclusion, recourse to state intervention implies that capital income bears no relationship to any productive service rendered and that distribution is not an objectively determined process. Finally, the traditional roles both of the consumer and producer are nullified: the consumer is no longer the final arbiter in the economic process, while the bourgeois capitalist ceases to be an efficient organizer of productive resources.

Thus, this initial bourgeois response to the crisis in economic thought involved, on its own terms, a very considerable degree of self destruction. Moreover, from the practical point of view, the bourgeois policy of state intervention was unsuccessful. In the first place the state proved to be totally inefficient as an organiser of capital, for the very good reason that the nature of capital is essentially private. And secondly, simple state intervention is quite unable to resolve the fundamental disequilibrium of the system—that of the alienation of the worker from his product—for this disequilibrium is rooted in the nature of material production associated with the capitalistic relationship.

On formal grounds, the response of bourgeois thought to its crisis was most odd, if perfectly understandable. It consisted of a complete rejection of the marginalistic framework and a return to the original concepts of bourgeois thought, in particular those associated with Physiocratic and Ricardian thought—a return in fact to the more 'naïve' concepts which arose from the recognition of a tri-partite class division of society. This position, which may be called neo-Ricardian, is not yet predominant in bourgeois thought, though it is making rapid process and its presence has brought about deep division within contemporary non-Marxist thought.

The profound limitation inherent in this reaction may be discerned from the fact that Ricardian theory, because of its own inadequacies, gave rise historically to two separate developments. The first of these, marginalism, was in direct opposition to Ricardian thought; the second, Marxism, was a positive and encompassing development of it. Bourgeois thought, in referring back to Ricardo through criticism of marginal theory, assumes that subsequent thought was diametrically opposed to Ricardo without there being any positive development, as was the case with Marx. Such a procedure in fact completely ignores the existence of Marxism, which latter makes a simple reference back to Ricardo alone impossible.

Thus, even on a formal level, bourgeois thought presents a totally inadequate reaction to its crisis. Moreover, the resolution of its inadequacies is particularly difficult because, as we shall see, the neo-Ricardian position is capable of presentation in Marxist, that is, non-bourgeois terms. We will later examine the historic root of this equivocation in more detail.

As previously mentioned, contemporary Marxist thought also finds itself in very obvious difficulties. I propose here to indicate some aspects of these, though I shall in the main consider the economic questions involved. Schematically, one may say that difficulties arise in three areas of Marxist thought: the theory of value, the theory of crisis, and the theory of new forms taken by capitalism.

As regards the theory of value, one does well to remember the central position it has in Marx's theory. It is in fact by means of value that Marx defines capitalism's historical function: capital is the unique and necessary generalization of mercantile production, by reducing all products into commodities by means of the reduction of labour itself into goods. In other words, capital is the universal value which makes society possible. Capitalist society, on account of its basis, is a collection of material relationships between persons and social relationships between things. This signifies that in Marx's thought the concept of capitalist society cannot be distinguished from the nature of value.

Various difficulties, however, arise in Marxist value theory, and take the following form: on the one hand value is the 'common substance' of goods and in this sense arises from a process of substantive creation; but on the other hand, the necessary expression of value is in exchange value because outside of exchange substantiation could not arise and would be meaningless. Now if the 'category' exchange value is rigorously developed until one arrives at its most immediate form, that of price of production, then the definition of the relationship between value as substance and value as exchange ratio give rise to a problem as yet unsolved. None of the solutions of the so-called 'transformation' problem have been deemed satisfactory.

That is why the neo-Ricardian position, which we have previously mentioned, can be seriously presented as a continuation of Marxism, even though it eschews the concept of value as a substance and thereby all Marxian analysis and understanding of capitalism.

So far as the theory of crisis is concerned, one can discern two different lines in Marx's thought. The first line makes reference to the contradiction between production and circulation, or, if one prefers, between the creation of surplus value and its market realization. The second line bears on the contradiction between the tendency for capital to substitute dead, or objectified labour for living labour and the same capital's tendency to keep living labour within the productive process because living labour is the source of surplus labour and surplus value. This second contradiction can also be expressed in terms of a substantial ambivalence in the relationship between objectified and living labour in so far as they together form capital: the end goal of capital is the maximization of objectified labour which places objectified labour in a position of paramount importance as compared with living labour; but, on the other hand, living labour is the agent of such maximization, and in this sense living labour assumes the supreme importance.

These two lines of thought form the basis of the Marxist representation of the capitalistic crisis. They refer to the realization crisis (overproduction or underconsumption) and to the tendency for the rate of profit to all. The associated problems involved, inconclusively discussed in Marxist thought, are of two types. Firstly, it is necessary to establish whether the realization crisis and the tendency for a falling rate of profit can be respectively considered as suitable and sufficient expressions of the two fundamental contradictions identified by Marx. Secondly, one must determine what relationships exist between the two contradictions, and their formulation in crisis terms. I believe Marx to have posed both these problems, but that their solution requires theoretic work which has only just started.

It is essential to bear in mind that, so far as Marx is concerned, the distinction between value theory and the theory of crisis is purely arbitrary. Nevertheless, the definition of such arbitrariness, as it illustrates the underlying unity of the two theories, is a valid question to explore. In this regard one may recall that, in the first place, the contradiction between production and circulation is simply an alternative way of expressing the contradiction between value and value in exchange. And so far as the second theory is concerned, the contradiction between the tendency to augment dead labour as compared to living labour and the tendency to retain living labour within the productive process is simply an alternative way of expressing the contradiction involved in reducing labour to value—or if one likes, to variable capital or labour power. Such contradiction implies that while variable capital forms but one part of total capital, variable capital is the agent which renders value to capital and hence is itself total capital.

As well as these problems, which can be regarded as traditional to Marxism (though the terminology employed in defining them is comparatively modern), there are further difficulties encountered arising from necessary attempts to establish relationships between different aspects of Marxist thought and actual features of neo-capitalist society. Such features include the chronic rather than cyclical nature of realization crises; the permanent nature of state intervention, for this and other reasons; the changing forms of imperialism, which have become more complex and subtle; the increasingly monopolistic nature of the market; and, finally, the ever widening distribution of income which has in some cases reversed the economic, political, and social support enjoyed by profits, such that costs have been imposed which have actually cut into profits.

But there is yet another question, which has become ever more urgent in Marxist thought, that of what form future societies are likely to take. This question has been prompted by the historic circumstances which have arisen. These are marked on the one hand by the 'maturity' of certain parts of capitalism, specified by the common presence of great productive development potential and insurmountable obstacles to such development, and on the other by the existence of societies born from revolution which are characterized by total state economic planning, albeit in different ways. In terms of Marx's thought, the question concerns the analysis of a society in which labour is immediately social, and the mediation of goods is not necessary for the establishment of society.

The particular problems which go to make up the overall question are manifold. Thus, how can one judge existing planning processes? What are their relationships to capital on the one hand and to future society on the other? In a future society, what is the meaning of 'non-capitalistic use of machines'? In very general terms how can one constitute or reconstitute the production and consumption (work and needs) units, which capital has set in conflict by its contradictory disassociating and unifying action on them?

To conclude, I must repeat that the foregoing is for reference only, as a guide to the many problems and difficulties presented by the contemporary state of economic science—problems which can appear discouraging on account of their complexity.

Two:

The Physiocrats

The Physiocrats made the economic system as a whole the subject of their inquiry, taking the economic system to be a single organism which was subject to necessary laws and which was therefore capable of scientific explanation. The premise underlying their argument is thus the assertion that a 'natural order' of society exists, an order analogous to that which rules the physical universe. The analogy, however, is not complete. The order of the physical universe* is objectively given and exists independently of man's will or intervention; but, according to the Physiocrats, the order of society exists only in as much as men desire it to exist and so do not oppose its introduction. In contrast to what happens in the physical universe, then, society may be far removed from its proper order. The proper order of society is defined as 'natural' only in the sense that if men do not oppose the free development of various forces which operate in society, society tends to shape itself according to a necessary design and to function in accordance with laws that are automatically incumbent on all.

For the Physiocrats, however, this is not the only difference between the order of society and the order of the physical universe. It is not simply a question of the existence or non-existence of the order of society. The 'natural order' of society is also the most desirable form of society since it confers on men advantages that they would not otherwise enjoy. We shall see later what these

* Quesnay had certainly discussed the theory of the circulation of the blood, and probably also the Newtonian theory of mechanics.

advantages are: meanwhile it can be seen that this outlook gives economic discussion not only the particular characteristic of observing and describing a given situation, but also that of passing judgement on it. Thus, a given situation can be compared with a paradigm which represents an optimum which could be attained if men would not mistakenly resist it.

The belief of the Physiocrats in a 'natural order' of society was without doubt connected with their awareness of the spread of the mercantile or merchant economy. It is important in this respect to show how the Physiocrats identified an element of the economic order—the general transformation of products into goods—as the basis of the 'natural order'. A collection of men forms a society, or rather an entity controlled by necessary laws, only in so far as the *economic* activities of men are integrated and brought together by a process that can be realized by exchange alone. We are thus confronted by an attitude that is almost an anticipation of the Marxist materialist interpretation of history, albeit in an extremely simple form when one considers all the differences between what is essentially an illuminating insight and a post-Hegelian inspiration.

There is no doubt, however, that the Physiocrats' point of departure in the field of economic analysis is the fact of exchange. As we shall see, the scientific explanation of the 'natural order' given by the Physiocrats refers to a purely mercantile economy. In this economy, as Quesnay says in a passage that clearly leads to Adam Smith: 'No man living in society can satisfy all his needs through his own labour; but he can obtain what he wants through the sale of the product of his labour',[1] and therefore as Mirabeau observes, 'Everyone labours for others, though he believes he is working for himself.'[2]

In order to explain the characteristics attributed to the 'natural order' of mercantilist society by the Physiocrats, it is necessary to bear in mind the picture of the economic process suggested by the actual economic structure of France in the middle of the eighteenth century. The economy was predominantly agricultural, and the ownership of land was generally aristocratic or feudal. The conditions of production in agriculture were typically capitalistic in the northern provinces where there was a well-defined class of capitalist farmers, while in the South peasant agriculture was still the rule. The manufacturing and commercial activities of the cities were very rarely capitalistic, being dominated by artisans and craft organizations. Comparisons of productivity showed capitalistic agriculture to have a net superiority over peasant agriculture.[3] This suggested to the Physiocrats the thesis that tenancies of the capitalistic type, entrusted to the responsibility and entrepreneurial capacity of bourgeois tenants, were the more advanced and more desirable of the two types of agricultural holding. The presence in the economy of non-capitalist organization thus came to be considered as a residuum associated with the near demise of feudalism: it was characteristic of a transitional phase that would necessarily evolve towards a general capitalistic order in the countryside. In the physiocratic schema it is always assumed that this transitional phase is over, and that capitalism has taken over the entire productive agricultural process. As far as the treatment of the activities of city-dwellers is concerned, however, this assumption does not hold: it is assumed that the natural form of organization here is based on an artisan structure. The physiocratic attitude to capitalism is thus quite remarkable—on the one hand it takes account of the great force for development of capitalism as an organizational form of the productive process, to the point of showing it to extend throughout all the sectors in which it has gained a foothold; on the other hand it appears that the particular economic structure facing the Physiocrats hindered them from seeing in manufacturing activity what were to be the greatest possibilities for the development of the capitalist order.

On closer inquiry, however, it can be seen that the structure of the French economy is not in itself sufficient to explain the limitations placed by the Physiocrats on the extent of the capitalist economy. Examples of capitalistic organization in manufacturing, though very rare, were certainly not entirely absent and should have suggested extensions of capitalistic organization similar to those carried out in agricultural activity. There is in fact a more important reason which explains the physiocratic attitude. According to these authors the historic task of capitalism consists in the enlargement of the surplus which it makes possible, and in this respect the presence of capitalism has a significance and takes on a real economic importance only in those activities in which surplus arises and hence may be enlarged. The characteristic physiocratic thesis, according to which surplus arises in agriculture alone, is therefore the foundation of the other thesis that capitalism is an order proper to agriculture alone. One must be careful here not to confuse these two propositions: it is not because agriculture alone is capitalistic that agriculture is the unique activity that produces a surplus. It is rather because the surplus exists in agriculture only that capitalism, as a means of enlarging the surplus, makes sense in agriculture alone. Thus only by reference to the physiocratic theory of the surplus can one discern the reason for the different ways in which the Physiocrats thought the economic order must be managed.

2

For the Physiocrats, as for all economists who accepted the term, the surplus (*net product*) is that part of produced wealth which exceeds the wealth consumed in the process of production. Its significance is that it is either the basis of a superior, more varied, and richer consumption than that which merely restores the labour expended in production, or it is the fount of investment in production which may then be carried out on an ever increasing scale. The introduction of the concept of surplus value implies three problems: its significance, its origin, and its allocation.

The question of the significance of the 'net product' is presented by the Physiocrats in its more primitive form. That is, they saw the surplus not as the difference between two magnitudes of value, but as the difference between two physical magnitudes. In general, since in any single productive activity the wealth produced and the wealth expended in production are made up of collections of different goods, the calculation of the difference between these two 'wealths' would imply their previous reduction to a homogeneous magnitude by giving values to all the goods concerned. Thus in general, the determination of the surplus can only be made within the ambit of a value theory.

A theory of value is entirely lacking in physiocratic thought, however, and they were therefore unable to perceive surplus in general—that is, in every sector—and saw it in one particular productive sector only, namely agriculture. This is because in agriculture *all* of the goods expended in the productive process (means of subsistence for the labourers, animal foodstuffs, and seeds) are found again in *larger* quantities in the collection of goods produced in this sector.[4] If one is limited, as the Physiocrats were, to considering only the physical aspects of production, rather than viewing production as the creation of values, then productive activity outside agriculture appears simply as a transformation of given objects into other objects. Productive activity in agriculture, however, manifests itself as a process that, starting with given objects, gives rise to a greater mass of objects of the same kind. Consequently all the surplus which the economy finds at its disposal became attributed to agriculture. However, even within this framework it is clearly necessary to have recourse to values, given that one does not wish to be limited simply to the recognition of the surplus but wants to go on to its quantitative determination also, to its measurement. For even in agriculture one cannot in general suppose that the proportionate mixes of goods are exactly the same in investment as in output. As we shall see, when the Physiocrats posed the problem of measuring the 'net product' in order to construct their quantitative schema, they resolved it empirically by accepting market prices as given. We shall also see what subsequent problems arose from this mode of procedure.

The solution to the problem of the origin of the surplus was suggested by the fact that the Physiocrats had recognized the surplus in agriculture alone. If the surplus indeed arises in that activity in which land intervenes as the determinant element of the productive process, this signifies that the power of creating 'net product' resides within the land itself. And this power cannot but depend on the fertility of the soil, as the result of which the product yielded by the land is greater than that necessary for reinvestment and for the means of subsistence of the labourers. If, following the Physiocrats, one defines as productive that labour which produces a surplus, one will then conclude that only agricultural labour is productive. One will also conclude that the productiveness of this labour does not depend on some particular characteristic distinguishing it from labour arising elsewhere, but on the fact that it is the type of labour that takes advantage of the natural fertility of the land.

The limitations of an approach which confines the formation of the surplus to agriculture, and which correspondingly considers agricultural labour alone to be productive, are evident. In the history of economic thought, however, the great significance of the physiocratic position is based on the identification of the *productive process* as the origin of the 'net product'. This achievement surpasses all previous conceptions which, in so far as they succeeded in distinguishing the surplus, saw its origin in the sphere of exchange and thus made it impossible to acquire an exact idea of the 'net product' phenomenon. The concept of surplus, in rigorous terms, was initiated by the Physiocrats and later developments in this field by the classical school—beginning with Smith—took the physiocratic theory as a natural point of departure.

Finally, where the question of the allocation of the surplus is concerned, the thesis that 'net product' is entirely resolved into the rent of land is characteristic of physiocratic thought (at least in Quesnay and Mirabeau). We have here another difference between Physiocracy and later classical theory. According to classical theory, 'net product' gives rise to two types of income, rent and profit; and it certainly appears strange that the physiocratic assumption of capitalistic agriculture was not accompanied by the recognition of profit as one of the surplus shares. Where manufacturing activity is concerned, it is natural that from the physiocratic point of view any income was considered labour income. It follows that any difference between the income earned by the master artisan and that collected by the ordinary labourer should be considered to be a difference attributable only to the different nature of the labour carried out, and to the different responsibilities assumed in the productive process. But where agriculture is concerned, the admission of the existence of the capitalist tenant should carry with it the recognition of profit as a specific income, paid from the surplus and commensurate with the capital invested. Instead, the income of the tenant came to be considered as part of the expenses of production and hence, when due allowance had been made for the type of labour performed, it was assimilated into the wages of agricultural labour. In this connection it would be pointless to look for greater coherence in the Physiocrats than that suggested by their thesis; one is dealing with an analytical deficiency that only later developments in the theory of capitalism were able to overcome. It is useful, however, to call attention to the fact that both Quesnay and Mirabeau recognized that capitalist tenants could *temporarily* share in the 'net product', so long as any of them succeeded, through improved production methods, in lowering their costs below prevailing levels. Such success, however, would only result in temporary incomes, since they are bound to be absorbed by rent with the first renewal of the leasehold, and hence the increased income accruing to the capitalist tenants cannot be regarded as a normal profit. It is also appropriate to bear in mind that Quesnay takes account of interest on invested capital, but that not even this interest is part of 'net product'. It is essentially conceived of as that part of total product that serves to renew fixed capital, and to cover maintenance costs, risks, and ill fortune.

3

This theory of surplus is the basis on which the school's founder Quesnay built his plan of the functioning of the economic system, the famous *Tableau economique*.[5] In this schema society is divided into three classes: (1) The 'productive' class, which is made up of all those—capitalist tenants and wage earners—who work in the agricultural sector, and whose labour is in fact productive in the Physiocratic sense of the term—that is by creating 'net product'. (2) The 'sterile' class, which is made up of all those who work outside agriculture, and whose labour is non-productive. It is in fact 'sterile' not because it is not useful, but in so far as it does not produce a surplus. (3) The third class is that of the landowners, who do not engage in any economic activity and who have the right to collect rent, which comprises all the 'net product'. This third class really includes the sovereign, including the court and all public servants, and the Church. They all receive a share of the rent, either in so far as they are themselves landowners—as is the case with the sovereign or the Church—or in so far as they have the right to collect taxes (the prerogative of the sovereign) or tithes (the prerogative of the Church).

Suppose that at the beginning of the year the productive class possesses all the agricultural products, and the sterile class all the manufactured products, of the previous year. The agricultural output of, say, 6 milliard monetary units is composed of foodstuffs valued at 3 milliards and raw materials worth 3 milliards. Suppose that this output has been produced through the investment of 3 milliards of *avances annuels* of annual capital (2 milliards for the labourers' subsistence—composed of 1 milliard of foodstuffs and 1 milliard of manufactures—plus 1 milliard of raw materials), together with the investment of 10 milliard of *avances primitives* or fixed capital which earns an annual 'interest' at 10 per cent of 1 milliard. This 'interest' is made up of goods produced by agriculture and is destined, as mentioned a little earlier, for the maintenance and renewal of fixed capital and a risk fund. The 'net product' is the difference between the 6 milliards of agricultural production and the 4 milliards of production expenses incurred, and is hence 2 milliards. The production of manufactures consists of goods worth 2 milliards, and it is assumed that this production has been obtained by means of an annual capital of 1 milliard for raw materials and through the consumption of 1 milliard of subsistence goods by the unproductive labourers. In addition, it is assumed that an amount of money equal to 2 milliards is initially in the hands of the productive class.

The problem of the *Tableau* is to determine how total wealth, initially accounted for, is redistributed between the three classes in such a way that: (1) income is paid to the rightful claimants; (2) conditions are produced such that both the productive and the sterile classes are able to repeat the production process on an unchanged scale.

The first step in the process of distribution is the transfer of 2 milliards from the productive class to the landowners for the payment of rent. The proprietors, in possession of this sum, first of all spend 1 milliard of it in order to acquire foodstuffs from the productive class, who thus receive back half of the sum of money originally at their disposal. The other milliard of rent will be expended by the proprietors in the acquisition of goods manufactured by the sterile class, which latter will use the money to buy foodstuffs from the productive class. The productive class therefore receive, once more, the other milliard that was initially in their possession. But they do not keep it, since it is spent on the sterile class so as to acquire manufactures destined for the subsistence of the productive labourers. The sterile class, in receipt of this milliard, spend it in turn on the productive class in the purchase of raw materials. Thus, all the money finally returns to the productive class, marking the end of the process of circulation of wealth between the classes.

In this process, then, the productive class have put 2 milliards of foodstuffs into circulation (giving 1 milliard of it to the landowners and 1 milliard to the sterile class) and also 1 milliard of raw materials. Of these 3 milliards of goods given up, 2 milliards correspond to rent and hence are lost to the productive class, while 1 milliard is offset by the purchase of 1 milliard worth of manufactures from the sterile class. In addition, the productive class has kept back for itself, from its own total product, 1 milliard of foodstuffs (which together with manufactures bought from the sterile class constitutes the consumption of the productive workers), 1 milliard of raw materials, and 1 milliard's worth of products corresponding to the 'interest' on fixed capital. Thus, so far as the productive class is concerned, having paid 'interest' on fixed capital (in the particular physiocratic sense) and having renewed all the working capital, conditions have been reproduced for a new productive cycle on the same scale as before. The sterile class, on the other hand, has given its 2 milliards of manufactured goods in exchange for 1 milliard of foodstuffs and 1 milliard of raw materials, and hence has also re-established the conditions for a new productive cycle of the same scale. Finally, the landowning class, having received 1 milliard's worth of foodstuffs from the productive class, and having made use of the remaining milliard of rent to buy manufactures from the sterile class, have had their proprietorial rights fully satisfied.[6]

4

The *Tableau* is the first general equilibrium analysis of the economic system, and for a long time remained the only one. For anything comparable one needs to look at Marx's 'reproduction' models more than a century later. As a representation of the actual economic process, the *Tableau* evidently possesses all the limitations inherent in the physiocratic standpoint. It is as well to emphasize that these limitations seem most serious when the conceptions involved are applied, with doubtful legitimacy, to a fully developed capitalistic economy, but that they appear to be less serious when one bears in mind the economic situation of pre-revolutionary France. We have already noticed deficiencies in the physiocratic analysis of economic classes, and it is easy to find them again in the mechanism described by the *Tableau*. For our purposes, however, it is more useful to show how Quesnay used the *Tableau* not only to describe reciprocal relationships and the general interdependence of economic phenomena, but also to illustrate the over-riding importance of the 'net product', because it is the 'net product' that determines the magnitude of the cycle described in the *Tableau*. The 'net product' is determined by the fertility of the earth and man's ability fully to exploit the natural powers of the soil using more advanced, that is capitalistic, methods of production in agriculture. In fact, as the *Tableau* shows, the entire process of circulation of wealth between the classes is set in motion by the payment of rent to the landowning classes, and the volume of exchange that takes place between the classes depends on the amount of such rent.

Now the Physiocrats give at least two reasons why a large rent formation is desirable. In the first place, through the maintenance of an important manufacturing activity, an ample rent signifies the possibility of considerably raising the level of consumption, if only for a given section of society, above mere subsistence. On this point there is certainly still present in the Physiocrats the old positive judgement on the excellence of feudal consumption. But, in the second place, an ample rent allows an enlargement of the economic process through investment of a part of the rent in the land (*avances foncières*). The possibility of increasing agricultural production by means of an increase in 'land' capital is considered on two occasions by the Physiocrats. First of all, with respect to that part of interest on the *avances primitives* which is set aside as a risk fund: they affirm that the utilization of this fund need not necessarily be postponed till such time as the circumstances against which one wished to be insured actually come about. It may in fact be used from year to year for the purpose of enlarging and improving the available land capital. However, the major source for this type of investment is the actual utilization of a part of the seigneurial rent which, by contrast, is predestined to be used in this way. It is made available through reductions of luxury expenditure (made to the sterile class) by the land proprietors every time that the land is incompletely or insufficiently cultivated, when essential or fixed equipment (buildings, roads, etc.) falls short or is insufficient for cultivation.

5

In this final physiocratic thesis there is undoubtedly a first representation of what was to become the central problem of classical economics, that of growth through accumulation or through the utilization of the surplus for capital formation. For a clear understanding of the physiocratic position and attitude it is necessary to add at once that the growth of agricultural production (and consequently of the entire system) which is obtained through the transformation of rent into capital is not, for the Physiocrats, a limitless process. The time must come when, to use Quesnay's expression, all the territory is 'cultivated to the highest degree' and hence 'landlords' rents can not be increased'.[7] At this point the accumulation process ceases and it would be pointless to transfer revenue from consumption purposes. We can now see clearly that the most plausible interpretation of Quesnay's approval of the level of *avances foncières* in the *Tableau* is that the *Tableau* itself relates to this stage of economic development, in which all the land has been subjected to the most efficient methods of production and the surplus is therefore at its maximum possible value.

But the extension of capitalistic tenancies throughout the land, as a way in which to adopt the most advanced methods of production, is not, according to the Physiocrats, the unique condition necessary to carry the economy to its highest level of production. There are at least three further conditions that must be met in this respect.

In the first place, it is necessary that no policy tends to lower the price of grain, for this would hinder agricultural production and so the formation of the 'net product'. In this respect the Physiocrats essentially refer to the necessity of abolishing restrictions, then prevalent in French political economy, on the export of grain; restrictions which, having regard to the productive capacity of the country, had the effect of lowering prices in the home market.

In the second place, it is necessary that the prices of manufactures be at their lowest possible level compatible with production costs, so that the real value of rent would be maximized. To this end, it is necessary to avoid all monopolistic situations in manufacturing activity, and above all to remove the (then numerous) barriers that, by impeding the free movement of goods within the country and hence fragmenting the national market, were hindering the full unfolding of free competition. This point of view, together with the previous one relating to the external grain trade, shapes that liberal attitude summarized in the formula *laissez-faire, laissez passer* that constitutes one of the most important characteristics of physiocratic thought.

Finally, it is necessary to have a type of tax system that does not bear down on production, and in particular does not hinder that renewal of circulating and fixed capital necessary to maintain a given level of production: from this arose the physiocratic proposition of an *impôt unique* on rent, perhaps the most radical of the reforms put forward by them, in so far as it is directly opposed to the maintenance of the traditional feudal right of tax exemption that the landowning class used to enjoy.

6

The situation described by the *Tableau* is thus one corresponding to the fulfilment of all the reforms proposed by physiocracy, which are, to summarize: an extension to all cultivatable land of capitalistic farming; the adoption, made possible in point of fact by the capitalistic structure, of the most advanced methods of cultivation and the setting up, for this purpose, of all the necessary land investments; the abolition of all restrictions on the export of grain in order that it may be guaranteed a *bon prix*; the elimination of all that works against a freely competitive market in manufactured goods; the setting up of a unique tax on rent, in place of all forms of tax that hinder the development of the productive process, lower efficiency, or increase costs.

In this sense the *Tableau* is the description of the *ordre naturel*. It is a description of the optimum situation, because the magnitude of the 'net product' is maximized, and hence the very amplitude of the entire economic process, and as such it is the standard according to which actual situations are judged. It is fitting to emphasize, in this respect, that the 'natural' character of this order is derived from the fact that its establishment should come about automatically, by inherent virtue of the free play of social forces, once the mistaken rules of government cease to obstruct the natural unfolding of such forces. It is also useful to note, in a critical vein, that while the physiocratic thesis had an obvious validity with regard to the consequence of a *bon prix* for grain and freely competitive price for manufactures, and while it was at least plausible as regards the attainment of high levels of production under the stimulus of capitalistic tenancies, it was not so obvious with regard to the extension of capitalistic tenancies throughout the land. In fact, in France at that time it was very doubtful whether such an extension could come about spontaneously. The fact that post-revolutionary French evolution especially favoured the spread of peasant ownership demonstrates the difficulties that would have been encountered by the physiocratic proposals.

7

Contradictions and difficulties revealed within the physiocratic schema presented a complex of unresolved questions that were left as an inheritance, so to speak, for later scientific inquiry.

First, we have seen that physiocracy has no particular theory of value and that the schema contained within the *Tableau* was therefore developed in detail by empirically accepting prices set in the market. Thus the size of the surplus is determined according to such prices, which, accepted as a datum, allows the comparison between the bundle of goods that make up the agricultural product and that which constitutes the annual cost incurred in its production. Now it is clear that, on the one hand, the acceptance of market prices as a datum implies the abandonment of a theoretical explanation of the formation of the 'net product'; but, alternatively, it is also evident that the Physiocrats were obliged to hold to such a course in the interpretation of the actual economy, because of the impossibility of carrying out the calculation of 'net product' in merely physical terms. As we have already pointed out, one cannot in general suppose that production inputs are composed of the same goods in the same proportions as outputs, thus making recourse to values indispensable even if agriculture were a closed world; not only that, but as the *Tableau* itself shows, not all the goods consumed by those who work in agriculture are produced by the agricultural sector, from which arises the necessity, so far as the demonstration of surplus is concerned, to account for the rates of exchange between agricultural products and manufactures. But if the determination of the surplus necessitates recourse to values in agriculture too, agriculture comes to lose that privileged position it holds if its production were of such a nature that allowed the calculation of the surplus in strictly physical terms.

This fact already raises doubts as to whether it is legitimate to restrict the search for the existence of 'net product' to agriculture. But there is another more important reason for disquiet. We have seen that the physiocratic schema admits that the entity of the 'net product' depends upon what we will now call the intensity of capital investment in land. If this is the case, however, it is no longer possible to attribute only to land, to its original and natural properties, the power of giving rise to a 'net product'; and we consequently come to abandon the main reason for limiting the phenomenon of surplus to agriculture alone. Finally, once the existence of a capitalistic structure has been recognized in a given sector (and if its general spread is hoped for), the resolution of the entire 'net product' into land rent becomes difficult to defend. One of the physiocratic theses is that the guarantee of a *bon prix* for grain is essential in order to establish a sufficient advantage for agricultural entrepreneurs to direct their efforts, in fact, to agriculture; and it is clear that such advantage is measured by comparing their income, not with their labour but with their capital. Thus, this income cannot be resolved into wages, and the question as to whether it is part of the surplus becomes of prime importance.

The line to be taken by economic thought immediately after physiocracy was one of research into the theory of value and as such would allow the quantification and generalization of *any* activity related to the phenomenon of the surplus. Such inquiry leads to a reformulation of the concept of 'productivity', and also the inclusion, within the surplus, of the income typical of the capitalistic economy, *viz*. profit.

References

1. The passage is taken from the article 'Grains', written for the *Encyclopedie*. See *François Quesnay et la physiocratie* published by the Institute national d'Etudes demographiques (Paris, 1958), vol. 2, *Textes annotés*, p. 506. See also the two translated extracts pp. 115–135 of the present work.

2. *Philosophie Rurale* (Amsterdam, 1764), op. cit., vol. I, p. 117.

3. According to data furnished by Quesnay in 'Grains', capitalistic agriculture (*grand culture*), while it took up one sixth of cultivated land, produced one quarter of the total output of grain (see *François Quesnay*, op. cit., p. 461).

4. This condition can be met when the economic system is considered as a whole, so long as production is represented as a 'circular process' (see P. Sraffa, *The Production of Commodities by means of Commodities*, Cambridge University Press, 1963). Such a method of procedure, however, was far beyond the scope of the Physiocrats.

5. The *Tableau* went through three editions during 1758–9 (see *François Quesnay*, op. cit., vol. 2, pp. 667–82). It was then republished with amplification and further comment by Mirabeau in collaboration with Quesnay in the *Analyse du Tableau Economique* (1766) and by other physiocratic writers.

6. There are several features of the schema that must be considered: (1) There is no interest on working capital, and it is obvious that so far as fixed capital is concerned, 'interest' is not really interest but a combination of an amortization and renewal fund, together with a sort of risk insurance premium. (2) The value of subsistence of the (unproductive) sterile class forms no part of any annual advance of working capital but is regarded instead as a current expense. Though the subsistence of the productive class is regarded as an advance of working capital there is no effect on the analysis, because working capital is assumed to bear no interest. (3) Again concerning the sterile class, there is no mention of investment in fixed capital, and consequently there is no renewal fund as there is for the productive class. On the other hand, one assumes that the working capital pertaining to the sterile class is entirely made up of raw materials and that the workers consume food only,

from which it follows that everything produced by this class is sold and nothing is left for itself. This did not appear to correspond to reality for some Physiocrats (*Baudeau*), who admitted the existence of an internal circulation for the sterile class, analogous to that which occurs for the productive class. (4) The economy considered by the *Tableau* is a closed economy, that is, without any external exchange relationships. As Quesnay recognized, since 'One can (only) buy from abroad exactly as much as one sells abroad,' total expenditure must always be equal to home production, and hence the consideration of foreign trade would not alter the working of the *Tableau*. One may add, following the suggestion of other interpreters, that if foreign trade is admitted it becomes clearer as to how the sterile class can obtain goods it needs, either for consumption or production. One could, in fact, suppose that part of the food bought from the productive class by the sterile class comes to be sold abroad in order to import manufactures.

7. *Analyse de la formule arithmetique du tableau economique* (1766), *François Quesnay*, op. cit., vol. 2, pp. 803–4.

Three:

Adam Smith

When Adam Smith taught moral philosophy at the University of Glasgow he divided his course into four parts: natural theology, ethics, rhetoric, and political economy. His two major works—the *Theory of Moral Sentiments* (1759) and the *Wealth of Nations* (1776) —can be regarded as a systematic exposition of the second and fourth parts of his teaching programme. The fact that these two works form part of the same schema poses the question of their interconnectedness, and in fact the understanding of Smith's economic theory (which is what concerns us here) is considerably facilitated when one takes into account relationships between the two.

Smith's moral philosophy is part of the development of eighteenth-century British thought that arose as a reaction to Hobbes' selfish system. Hobbes' system was based on his assertion of a state of nature in which all human behaviour is entirely motivated by self preservation, or selfishness. If this kind of individual behaviour were allowed unrestrained free play the end result, according to Hobbes, would be a universal and disruptive state of war between all men. For our purposes, it is important to emphasize the consequences that this brand of moral philosophy has in the field of political theory, consequences that were traced out with extreme rigour by Hobbes. If selfishness is the only natural basis of human activity, it must follow that society would be impossible without coercive state intervention. In other words political organization is not simply concerned with the organization of a society that has emerged from the natural and spontaneous tendency of men to build up a web of stable reciprocal relationships; it is rather the means that men, driven by fear, must employ to counteract the natural tendency towards dispersion; it is in fact the very source of social life. In the natural order of things it is logically impossible that a civil society could precede the state. Society can only arise by the institution of a state authority, and only in so far as men give up their personal freedom, which according to Hobbes is centrifugal and destructive in nature, in favour of state authority, no matter what form it takes.

Hobbes' pessimistic moral and political philosophy, based on the assumption of the essentially malevolent character of men's nature, provoked an intellectual reaction which was highlighted by the contributions of Locke and Hume. There is, however, much disagreement between Locke and Hume and a consideration of their differences helps towards an understanding of Smith's position in the field of moral and political thought.

One point that Locke has in common with Hobbes is his exposition of the problem on the basis of a natural state. This is a metaphysical residuum in Locke's thought that runs counter to his general empirical approach. Locke's state of nature, however, leads him to conclusions that are directly opposed to Hobbes' pessimism: according to Locke the state of nature is essentially good, and any conflicts that arise are not the consequences of man's natural wickedness, but instead result from a 'miserliness' of nature as manifested by an insufficiency of natural resources. A consequence of such scarcity is that not everybody can acquire property through his own labour, and hence some will seek to expropriate the property of others in order to establish themselves. Thus the existence and continuation of civil society, though based upon the social and co-operative character of man, is constantly threatened by pressures which arise from the 'niggardliness' of nature. The state does not appear to Locke as the fount of civil society, but as the guarantor of its permanence, as an organ that protects property by the force of law, and which therefore allows the natural order to come to fruition. State authority does not, as Hobbes thought, imply an alienation of individual liberty, but is rather the instrument through which liberty can be fully defined and protected from any attack or emergence of disorder.

Locke's system contains a difficulty which he is unable to overcome, or rather which he implicitly resolves by excluding any democratic ideal from his brand of strict liberalism. The state, in its role as the protector of civil society, cannot mitigate that paucity of natural resources which promotes disruptive tendencies. Inevitably, then, Locke's society must contain within it 'have nots' whose existence can only be justified if one supposes them to be less capable than others of acquiring property through their own efforts. His system is consistent only if, in conjunction with the bounty of nature, one assumes there to be an essential natural inequality between different men. Precisely because it is natural, this inequality is insuperable, and it is therefore unthinkable that one of the state's duties should be to overcome it. English liberalism, as associated with Locke, was hence strictly of the bourgeois variety and it is important to remember this when we come to examine Smith's thought.

There is an even more profound difficulty in Locke which is absolutely insuperable given the context of his philosophy. Locke's state of nature is dominated by a law of reason: against the irrationalism of Hobbes' natural state of strife and discord, Locke puts forward the concept of a rational law which at times he traces back to the Deity. Now the consistent development of such an approach can only be along rationalistic lines—which is inconsistent with his empirical method. That is to say, having accepted Hobbes' point of departure, the only way in which to reject Hobbes' conclusions is to hypothesize a law of reason that governs the natural state, and then go on to analyse the relationships between natural and *positive* laws. But when according to Locke's doctrine the origin of cognition is in sensible experience this kind of procedure is inadmissible, for it is impossible adequately to define a *rational* law that rules the state of nature. Consequently, the criticism that Locke provides us with *vis-à-vis* Hobbes' *bellum omnium contra omnes* is couched in terms of a hypothesized natural tendency towards happiness, which if admitted would completely negate Hobbes' conclusions. The empirical evidence for the existence of any such tendency is completely lacking: man does not exist in a state of nature and never has. There is thus a dichotomy in Locke between a rationalistic approach, initially accepted by him but not developed, and an empirical approach that comes to dominate the development of his ideas but which is contradictory to his original premise.

British philosophical thought was not able to offer a rationalistic criticism of Hobbes' philosophy. It developed instead on the basis of a radical rejection of the state of nature concept and a full use of the empirical approach. Hume's contribution is the apogee of this movement. According to Hume a major flaw in 'philosophical egoism' is that any definition of the law of reason it offered was without cognitive validity; Hume's approach was via the examination of man's psychology, which led him to believe in the existence of a 'sentiment' that, as opposed to selfishness, is associated with a desire to do that which is good, in the sense of affording utility or pleasantness to others, and being conducive to social harmony.

According to Hume, an analysis of what society deems to be virtuous behaviour leads one to the conclusion that such behaviour is characterized by its usefulness, in the sense that it is geared towards the interest of the individual or society. This is where Hume's 'sentiment' opposed to selfishness comes in, which he calls 'benevolence', 'humanity', or 'sympathy', and which is the basis of 'moral judgements'—those judgements that approve of 'virtue', that is, everything useful to the individual or society. 'Humanity' or 'sympathy' is the point of origin of virtuous behaviour, for it motivates individuals to work for the good of others as the best means to achieve advantageous reciprocal social relationships. Selfishness precludes individual recognition of interpersonal utility, but Hume recognized in man a 'human sympathy', according to which the individual considers not only his own utility, but that of others as well.

Thus Hume's thought offers the greatest possible vindication of moral autonomy that empiricism is able to afford; man's moral facilities provide an appropriate evaluatory vehicle for other aspects of human life, particularly in the political field. Nevertheless the development of various pointers in Hume's system is impossible unless one goes outside his 'empiricism', primarily because a methodological framework based on actual psychological sense impression is inadequate for an analysis of the fundamental moral concept of 'duty'. Such a concept involves the kind of approach attempted a little later by Kant. Staying within the confines of pure empiricism we encounter a difficulty which is implicit in Hume, and which had already been made sufficiently explicit by Hutcheson, who was Smith's teacher at the University of Glasgow. Hutcheson argues for the independent, non-derivative nature of the 'moral sense', and his demonstration that all human behaviour is ultimately traceable to the quite original natures of egoism and altruism, brought to light a fundamental dualism in men's psychological made up. Empiricism can scarcely resolve this dichotomy in human motivation, because within its methodological framework such conflicting sentiments can only be regarded as ultimate data and as such incapable of further analysis.

Nor could these philosophers conclude that egoism can be identified with evil and altruism with good. In the first place it is an absurdity to derive a moral code on an empirical basis, and then use that code to pass moral judgements on itself; and secondly 'egoism' as defined was by no means exclusive of 'virtue' in so far as the creation of social life is concerned. Mandeville's famous *Fable of the Bees* had suggested connections between egoism and social life as far back as the beginning of the eighteenth century. Mandeville's analysis showed that unless individuals were selfishly motivated and egoistical social life would come to a halt, particularly as regards the process of the acquisition of wealth: civilization, at least from the materialistic point of view, is a product of selfishness.

The impossibility of separating cause from effect when analysing the workings of self interest on society emphasized the need to reconsider the relationships between the state and politics, an area of thought that had, with Hume, all but disappeared from the realm of philosophical speculation. In particular, the lack of analysis of the workings of self interest excluded the possibility of explaining the existence of the state on the basis of needs present in a state of nature. Also, if Hume's principle of morality—the exercise of altruism—came to be regarded as encompassing all aspects of behaviour and all free will, moral autonomy may be indicated, but it can hardly be used as a starting point for the explanation of political and constitutional reality.

What follows from all this is the need to create a basis from which the political problem(s) discussed by Locke can be tackled, a basis which incorporates the empiricist, Humeian explanation of morality but which does not rely on a rationalization methodology. The attribution of a positive social role to egoism can be exploited in this context, and such a procedure characterizes Smith's contribution.

The dualism in the psychological make up of man is deliberately treated by Smith as, in some respects, a very important subject of philosophical inquiry. The most interesting aspect of the *Theory of Moral Sentiments* is the fact that Smith, having confirmed utility in Hume's sense as the foundation of morality, specifies an area of self-interested human behaviour which is justified by the same utility principle. Self interest operates in the economic sphere, where everyone freely strives for the maximum advantage in exchange, and their efforts result in the maximization of social wealth. The peculiar dichotomy in British psychological ethics was thus crystallized but, at the same time, in a sense, resolved. For the separation of human activity into two spheres, a moral sphere in which societal utility is derived from the exercise of sympathy, and an economic sphere in which utility is consequent upon individual self interest, made it possible to avoid conflict between selfishness and humanity. Mandeville's 'private vices', which through the mechanism of production and exchange could be transformed into 'public virtue', were not in fact vices according to Smith, not even on an individual level, but were rather positive tendencies so long as they operated in the appropriate sphere.

The main point of Smith's thesis is that selfishness need not be a disruptive element in society, but can instead be conducive to order and development: 'can' in the sense that for selfishness to have a positive social effect, a necessary condition must be fulfilled. This is that individuals, in pursuing their self interest, do not obstruct others in the pursuit of theirs, that there is no abuse of power based upon natural positions of strength or institutional privileges. In this sense the *Wealth of Nations* represents a systematic attempt to explain how, so long as the necessary condition is met, the unfettered economic behaviour of individuals gives rise to the constitution and development of the socio-economic structure. One can say that so far as British philosophy is concerned, Hume provided the justification for moral autonomy, and Smith justified economic autonomy. Economic autonomy in Smith's schema is the very foundation of civil society, and as such is the basis of its actual organization. Hence his call for the guarantee of an institutional framework within which systematic production, exchange, and consumption can take place. As we shall explain more fully later, Locke's bourgeois liberalism was supported by Smith's contribution, but we shall see that Smith had a greater awareness as regards what one may properly define as the democratic problem, of how the enlargement of the economic society could systematically reduce the number and burden of the 'have nots'.

2

To evaluate the argument contained in the *Wealth of Nations*,[1] it is useful to bear in mind that the economic ideas of Smith had been previously expressed in the *Glasgow Lectures*. Our knowledge of the Lectures is based on the notes taken by a student in 1763 and subsequently published by E. Cannan in 1896.[2] Three aspects of the *Lectures* are worthy of mention here.

In the first place, the economic environment that Smith sets out to analyse is essentially based on the independent labourer—that is to say the *artisan*—who can combine with a given number of other workers from whom he is distinguished only by the greater responsibility he assumes in the organization of the productive process. Unlike the capitalist, the artisan does not have an economic role that is distinct from that of the labourer. Thus, Adam Smith confronts us with a society that, though fully mercantilist, is not yet capitalistic.

Secondly, Smith does not identify profit as a specific form of income, and the income level of the master artisan is compared with his work input and not with the capital he advances. In this respect, Smith's position in the *Glasgow Lectures* is analogous to that of the Physiocrats, though he is more justified in this than were the latter who were concerned with an agricultural organization of production that was already fully capitalistic.

Thirdly, the *Lectures* contain an outline of the theory of value which, in particular, distinguishes between market price and 'natural price', a distinction that we meet again in the *Wealth of Nations*. This is followed by a description of the mechanism that systematically reduces market price to 'natural price'. Given the nature of the economic conjuncture considered in the *Lectures*, the 'natural price' of a good must be resolved into the 'natural price' of the labour necessary to produce it. Smith defines the 'natural price' of labour as that which 'is sufficient to maintain [a man] during his time of labour, to defray the expense of education, and to compensate the risk of not living long enough, and of not succeeding in the business'.[3] The mechanism which tends to equate the market price of a good with its 'natural price' is that of competition, which is naturally conceived of as a competition between workers. There is a tendency for workers to flock into those trades where, because the market price of the products is higher than their natural price, wages are higher, and to abandon those where the reverse is the case.

These three features of Smith's economic theory as expounded in the *Glasgow Lectures* were short lived, and destined to give way to alternative concepts and formulations when he came to offer a theory of a capitalistic economy. There was, however, another element in the *Lectures* destined to become a permanent feature and characteristic of Smith's thought (in so far as it was introduced by him), and which is in fact a perfectly general feature of economic activity and as such independent of any particular historical setting. It concerns the identification of the cause that determines the progressive increase of the 'productivity' of labour.

According to Smith increasing labour productivity is due to the *division of labour*, that is to the progressive reduction of the number of different productive operations executed by a single labourer. At the one extreme we have the situation in which each labourer undertakes *all* the productive operations necessary to the production of his subsistence, and at the other, a situation in which he carries out *only one* such operation. Going from one extreme to the other evidently requires an increasingly strict social integration between the various workers, in the sense that each one must enter into exchange relationships with an increasing number of others in order to be able to satisfy his consumption needs. According to Smith there are three reasons why the division of labour leads to an increase in labour productivity, and his position is already clear in the *Lectures*. In the first place, the labourer's skill increases when he is able to concentrate on a relatively small number of operations, and reaches a maximum when he performs one operation only. Secondly, the smaller is the number of different operations performed by each worker, the less is the time wasted in changing from one operation to another. And finally, the more is activity restricted to fixed single operations the easier becomes the invention of machinery by means of which labour productivity is increased.

Smith, however, does not confine himself to identifying the division of labour as the cause of increased productivity; he also inquires why the division of labour came about in the first place. He denies that it is due to a natural diversity of talent and genius between men. On the contrary, he posits that men are born equal and that diversity, far from being natural, is a characteristic consequence of the division of labour. According to Smith, the origin of the division of labour can be traced to a propensity to exchange and barter, which is unique to man. It is by virtue of this propensity that men enter into a structure of social relationships which, through specialization, leads to ever greater exchanges of surplus products.

One finds this analysis repeated, almost unchanged, in the *Wealth of Nations*. The *Lectures*, however, consider an even more basic question, even if only by implication, *viz.*: on what is the propensity to exchange based? On this point, Smith comments in the *Wealth of Nations*, 'Whether this propensity be one of those original principles in human nature, of which no further account can be given; or whether, as seems more probable, it be the necessary consequence of the faculties of reason and speech, it belongs not to our present subject to inquire'.[4] But in the *Lectures* he had been more explicit, and affirmed that the real foundation of the tendency to exchange is found in the fact that there is an inherent need in man 'to persuade'. It is from this natural—and therefore inevitable—propensity for spiritual commerce, for the exchange of ideas, that Smith makes spring the tendency to trade and the exchange of material riches. Thus, commercial exchange is based upon a 'method' that men had originally cultivated for the exchange of products of reason.[5] What the *Wealth of Nations* had put forward as merely the more likely reason for exchange, the *Lectures* asserted as a certainty: the propensity to exchange material wealth (and therefore the division of labour on which is based on it) is not an original principle in human nature, but is 'the necessary consequence of the faculties of reason and speech'. There is no change of opinion in the *Wealth of Nations*; it is merely a matter of the emphasis placed on a question that Smith did not consider to be relevant in the restricted field of economic discourse. Nevertheless, this problem is not without importance, especially if one bears in mind the Smithian thesis put forward earlier, according to which the pursuit of personal interest in the production of wealth leads to the advantage of all concerned. The particular advantage gained is determined according to the division of labour, since if it is in one's personal interest to specialize and to increase one's productivity and hence to increase personal wealth through the exchange of one's ever growing surplus of goods, this process must result in greater social production, and therefore in an augmentation of general prosperity.

The *Lectures* specify that this process whereby wealth is increased through the spread of exchange has its roots in man's natural *rationality*; or rather that man, in so far as he is endowed with reason communicable through speech, can fully realize his nature only if he allows all his activities to be governed by the rule of communication and exchange. The isolation of the individual in the Hobbesian natural state of strife yields to the propensity, inherent in every one, to search out one's fellows as necessary for one's personal development; and the pessimistic vision of an essentially disintegrative natural state gives way to an optimistic vision of a natural state leading to mutual integration. This profound sense of harmony as a fact of nature permeates all Smith's work, and is a constant background to all his specific arguments.

How far has actual historical experience, according to Smith, been consistent with this natural harmony? As we shall see, we already find in Smith a warning of non-concordance between the natural and the actual state of things. Smith realized that history poses complex problems in this respect, problems that Ricardo later emphasized, concerning the effects of historically determined institutions, and elements of strife and disharmony that Smith had excluded from his vision of the natural state.

3

Before going into this question, which was to be of decisive importance in the history of classical British thought, it is necessary to examine how Smith moved from an analysis of a substantially pre-capitalistic to a capitalist economy.

It seems probable that, between 1763 and 1776, a combination of two factors caused Smith to change his field of analytic inquiry. The first of these must have been the phenomenon during this period of the increasing spread and strengthening of capitalistic industry in the cities (including Glasgow), which was coming to transform the entire economic way of life of the country. Features of particular relevance in this respect are on the one hand the predominance of wage labour as compared with independent labour, and on the other the associated competitive behaviour that was becoming adopted. It was through competition that Smith saw the tendency of market price to equal 'natural' price, and the competitive process seemed to be increasingly dominated by mutual competition between capitalists in search of the most remunerative investments for their capital, rather than labourers in search of more remunerative trades. Faced by such a real world situation, concepts used in the *Lectures*, at least up to a point, cannot have seemed entirely relevant. The second factor that must have had an influence in Smith's change of view was his contact with the Physiocrats during his visit to France of 1765 and 1766. The importance of this visit has been variously interpreted in the history of thought. On the one extreme some interpretations have considered as decisive to the development of Smith's thought the first analysis of the capitalistic process as made by the Physiocrats. At the other interpretative extreme, it has been considered that the influence of the Physiocrats would have had an opposite effect in so far as Smith, who was already aware of the importance of capitalism, would have had to direct Physiocratic thought towards an analysis of a more realistic conjuncture than that considered by Quesnay and Mirabeau. We do not intend to enter into the details of this question here; it does, however, seem reasonable to assert that Smith, having arrived in France with an awareness of the problems posed by the new economic reality, found some concepts in physiocratic theory that could certainly be taken as points of departure in a systematic development of theoretic tools relevant to the new economic system. At least two physiocratic concepts could be used for this purpose, even though only, as we have said, as points of departure. The first is the 'net product' concept, from which may be developed an income theory that recognizes the existence of income types that are distinct from labour income; and the other is the concept of 'advances', from which one may go on to construct a theory of capital.

We have shown above how physiocratic analysis displayed limitations and serious deficiences. It will be useful briefly to recall these defects here, so as better to appreciate the decisive advance that Smith had already made. Though the Physiocrats had a clear conception of the net product as a residual income, which would be maximized when production was organized on strictly capitalistic lines, they yet identified the net product with land rent, to the exclusion therefore of profit itself, or of the income that is typically associated with capitalism. Correspondingly, although 'advances' have their proper place in capitalistic activities, they are not related to profit in the physiocratic schema, but are simply seen as a particular form of wage payments; and the phenomenon of investment, the original phenomenon of capital, is seen as limited to agricultural investment to the exclusion of all other industrial activity. One can trace all these defects more or less directly back to the physiocratic concept of productivity, or rather to the importance they attached to the 'net product'. If in fact productivity can only exist through the natural attributes of the soil, if labour can only produce an income surplus to its subsistence needs because of the original fertility of the land, then (1) the production of the net product is possible only in agriculture, (2) consequently, it is only in agriculture that labour, via advanced capitalistic organization, can systematically augment the capacity to produce the net product inherent in land's natural fertility, (3) the net product belongs entirely to the landowner, who appropriates it all in the form of rent, (4) capital, which must be regarded as essential in giving rise to increased labour productivity, and hence to the net product, is nevertheless thought of as being quite separate from the *original* cause that creates the net product; as a consequence capital, in the physiocratic scheme of things, could not be adequately analysed let alone considered as a factor that is itself in part responsible for the formation of the net product—that part of it in fact which resolves itself in the form of profit.

Smith, while welcoming any physiocratic suggestions (in particular, as we have said, those implicit in the ideas of 'net product' and capital 'advances') overcomes the limitations and contradictions of the physiocratic scheme through his modification of their point of departure, that is, the concept of productivity. Clearly he did not deny that land was capable of spontaneous production independent of human intervention; but *in accepting the physiocratic definition of productivity as the power to create net product* he was led to assert that this power resides in labour and labour only. According to Smith, there is no *unique* factor separate from labour, which is the original source of productivity. Rather, *anything* (including, in particular, the fertility of land) which contributes to the net product which results from labour expenditure must be regarded as productive.

The attribution to labour of the ability to create net product led to the recognition that nearly all branches of industry are also capable of its creation. Smith considered net product a phenomenon as general as labour itself, and in this respect no one sector can be raised above any other because labour can be productive in whichever sector it is expended.[6] But this means that net product does not consist of rent only, and that it is no longer possible to follow the physiocratic supposition that the net product must be considered as accruing to the landowner. If in fact net product emerges due to the productivity of labour in sectors in which the fertility of land plays no part, then that part of the product which is surplus to the maintenance and reproduction of labour constitutes an income that clearly reflects the fact that an advance of capital is generally necessary for the maintenance of such labour. And, because such an advance by a capitalist is necessary, the capitalist claims a share in the product of labour in the form of profit. Even in agriculture, only part of the net product accrues as rent to the proprietor; a share of it is taken by the capitalist, depending on the size of the advance he makes. On the other hand, profit cannot, as claimed by the Physiocrats, be considered a special form of labour remuneration, simply distinguished from normal wages on a quantitative rather than a qualitative basis. This is clearly shown in the *Wealth of Nations*, for the decisive reason that a given profit is compared not with the task, say, of inspection and direction undertaken by the capitalist, but with the amount of capital he has advanced.[7]

It is in this way that the kind of economic society that Smith sets out to analyse in the *Wealth of Nations* takes shape. One is dealing with a society in which total national product, in so far as it is a consequence of productive labour, can be broken down into three parts: the first of these is the wage element, that provides for the maintenance and reproduction of labour; the other two parts taken together, correspond to the 'net product' of the Physiocrats, which nowadays we would describe by the term 'surplus'. Both these latter two parts are termed 'deductions from the produce of labour' by Smith and consist of first, the *rent* of the landlord and, secondly, the *profit* of the master or, in more modern terminology, of the capitalist.[8] Smith does not deny the possibility of cases in which 'a single independent workman has stock sufficient to purchase the materials of his work, and to maintain himself till it be completed'; in which case 'He is both master and workman, and enjoys the whole produce of his labour.' But he asserts that 'such cases are not very frequent, and in every part of Europe, twenty workmen serve under a master for one that is independent'.[9] Such cases, which already appeared of little importance to Smith, are thus excluded from his schema, within which normal production gives rise to three social groups, or *ranks*, of society: the wage earners, landlords receiving rent, and capitalists receiving profit. The primary problem that Smith sets himself is the analysis of the causes that influence the productivity of labour and the distribution of total product between the three ranks of society (the title of the first book of the *Wealth of Nations* is: 'Of the Causes of Improvement in the productive Powers of Labour, and of the Order according to which its Produce is naturally distributed among the different Ranks of the People').

As regards 'the causes of improvement in the productive powers of labour' Smith, as we have already indicated, once again takes up the same arguments he had earlier put forward in the *Lectures* concerning the division of labour. We will not, therefore, repeat such arguments here, but instead confine ourselves to pointing out that the *Wealth of Nations* was much more explicit with respect to the role capital plays in increasing the division of labour and hence enhancing productivity. In essence Smith says that capital, by bringing together a large number of workmen, enables there to be a more 'proper division and distribution of employment', and can supply the labourers with the 'best machinery'.[10] As Smith himself recognized, it is because of this aspect of capitalistic organization that capitalism was destined to supersede an economic system based on the independent labourer.

On the question of the distribution of the product, Smith was faced by a problem that the Physiocrats had been able to avoid owing to their supposition that the only productive labour was that expended in agriculture. We have already gone into the reasons why, in the physiocratic setting, the attempt to define net product in purely physical terms seemed plausible—without any recourse, that is, to a theory of value. We have also seen how, remaining within the physiocratic framework, no difficulties arose as a result of this procedure. Quite insuperable problems, however, would arise when productivity is attributed to labour as Smith assumed, rather than to the natural fertility properties of the soil. When one generalizes from agriculture to all the other industrial activities that make up the economy, we have no reason to suppose that the goods used as the means of production are the same as the goods that emerge as the gross product; and still less to suppose that the proportionate mix of goods that comprise the input is the same as the output. In other words to arrive at the quantitative determination of the net product it is necessary to express the input and total output in like terms, or in value terms. Thus, the formulation of a theory of value becomes an integral and indispensable part of the theory of distribution.

4

The problem, as is well known, is introduced by the following proposition: 'Every man is rich or poor according to the degree in which he can afford to enjoy the necessaries, conveniences, and amusements of human life. But after the division of labour has once thoroughly taken place, it is but a very small part of these with which a man's own labour can supply him. The far greater part of them he must derive from the labour of other people, and he must be rich or poor according to the quantity of that labour which he can command, or which he can afford to purchase. The value of any commodity, to the person who possesses it and who means not to use or consume it himself, but to exchange it for other commodities, is equal to the quantity of labour which it enables him to purchase or command. Labour, therefore, is the real measure of all commodities.' And a little later: 'Labour was the first price, the original purchase-money that was paid for all things. It was not by gold or silver, but by labour, that all the wealth of the world was originally purchased; and its value, to those who possess it, and who want to exchange it for new productions, is precisely equal to the quantity of labour which it can enable them to purchase or command.'[11]

We will return later to Smith's definition of value as *labour commanded* in an attempt to discover its true significance. But first of all we draw attention, on strictly analytical grounds, to the nature of the problem posed by such a measure of value. *Labour commanded* itself evidently depends upon exchange value—that is, on the value of labour or the wage rate. Thus, though *labour commanded* raises no difficulties as a *measure* of the value of goods, and hence of the use of the wage rate as a unit of account, it cannot be assumed, without reasoning in a circle, that *labour commanded* is the *determining* element of exchange values. That Smith was aware of this problem is clearly shown by the fact he himself asked how *labour commanded*, in its turn, was determined.

The reply that Smith gave to this question divides itself into two parts. He first of all starts with the assertion 'in that early and rude state of society which precedes both the accumulation of stock and the appropriation of land, the whole produce of labour belongs to the labourer; and the quantity of labour commonly employed in acquiring or producing any commodity, is the only circumstance which can regulate the quantity of labour which it ought commonly to purchase, command or exchange for'.[12] We may hence summarize: in the primitive conditions hypothesized by Smith, the quantity of *labour commanded* is equal to the quantity of labour embodied, when the latter is taken to mean the quantity that was necessarily employed in the production of a given good. But the situation changes when one moves from the primitive stage, in which all of labour's product belongs to the labourer, to a stage where the value of a good is made up not only of wages, but also profit which arises through the accumulation of capital, and rent resulting from the private appropriation of land. In this case, the quantity of labour that a good can command will correspond to the value of rent and profit, that is, the value of the surplus, as well as the value of the labour embodied. Consequently, when we leave the primitive stage, we can no longer say that *labour commanded* is equal to labour embodied.

The question as to whether Smith was correct when he supposed it to be impossible to use labour embodied in a commodity as being equal to its value will be discussed later, when we consider the Ricardian criticism of Smith. Here we will limit ourselves to noting the conclusion arrived at by Smith, and take up his development of the second part of the value question, *viz.*: what determines the quantity of labour that a good may command in exchange? Since the price of a good 'finally resolves itself' into wages, profit, and rent, and since 'the real value of all the different component parts of price, it must be observed, is measured by the quantity of labour which they can, each of them, purchase or command',[13] it follows that the quantity of *labour commanded* by the good is determined by the levels of wages, of profit, and of rent. Moreover, since the competitive process gives rise to a given 'ordinary or average rate' of wages, profit, and rent—rates that are called 'natural' by Smith and which systematically tend to prevail over temporary market fluctuations—the quantity of labour which, in equilibrium, a good can command is determined by the 'natural price'[14] of that good: that is, the price that holds when the natural rates of wages, profit, and rent are paid to the factors of production used in its manufacture.

One evidently encounters a problem with this conception of the elements that make up *labour commanded*: the natural rates of wages, profit, and rent are themselves values, and hence it becomes necessary to determine how they, in turn, are determined. Smith, then, did not succeed in furnishing a theory of value that satisfied the necessary formal requirement that its elements do not themselves depend upon values. *In this sense*, therefore, there can be no doubt that Smith's theory of value is a failure: the problem of the determination of relative values, the solution of which depends on the ability to evaluate the surplus or net product, remains unsolved. There is, however, a sense in which Smith's theory of value, though being a failure, constituted a decisive stage in the history of economic thought. As we shall see, the realization of its significance required that the *labour commanded* criterion became considered in the context of the theory of capitalistic growth (along lines Smith himself suggested) rather than in the context of the determination of exchange value. It thus became used as a criterion for the recognition and measurement of growth itself. However, before taking up this point, it is useful to consider two questions of great theoretic importance that Smith dealt with in his theory of exchange.

The first question concerns the nature of profit and rent. As we have previously said, Smith defines both rent and profit as deductions from the product of labour.[15] The landowner and capitalist are able to effect such deductions because of land-ownership by the one, and capital advances for the maintenance of labour during the production period by the other. We are now able to specify that the relevance of this definition rests upon the fact that it anticipates the theory, that was to be fully developed by Marx, according to which the surplus is a result of *labour-surplus*. *Labour-surplus* is the amount of labour rendered by the labourers over and above that necessary for their subsistence. It is important to note that this conception of the surplus is fundamental for the generalization to a capitalistic economy of the theorem that *labour embodied* is a determining factor of exchange value, a generalization that was attempted by Ricardo and Marx, but one which Smith did not deem possible.

The second question concerns the idea that all prices are resolvable into wages, profit, and rent. Here, we can bear in mind that though Smith, as we have said, asserts that the resolution of price into these three constituent parts occurs only finally (hence allowing us to suppose that other factors apart from the three mentioned could be present, which we could go on to analyse) he sometimes reasons as if values were *directly* composed of wages, profit, and rent. As if, that is, wages profit and rent *currently* paid exhaust the value of a good, and that one need not also take into account those wages, profit, and rent previously paid in producing the means of production, the value of which latter must enter into the good's price. Thus, for example, he always identifies the annual value of national production as the sum of incomes distributed during the same year in the form of wages, profits, and rent.

5

Having cleared up these points, we can now see in what sense the Smithian concept of *labour commanded* became relevant in the field of economic growth theory. We begin by showing that even though *labour commanded*, for the reasons given above, cannot be considered as the factor that determines exchange values, it can nevertheless perfectly well be used to measure such values. In particular, it can be used as a measure of that part of value corresponding to the surplus. Moreover we can state that for Smith *labour commanded*, used as a measure, came to acquire a significance that went well beyond what one might have supposed. We know that according to Smith labour is productive when it produces a value in addition to its means of subsistence (the surplus being appropriated in the forms of profit and rent); now we are enabled to state definitely that it is labour productivity which gives rise to a net product such that *labour commanded* is greater than labour embodied. Therefore, as compared with labour embodied, *labour commanded* is not limited simply to giving us a measure of the value of a good, but can also be said to measure the contribution that the good in question could make to an increase in general production through an increase in employment. Smith regards this as only a possibility, since the fact that *labour commanded* is greater than labour embodied does not in itself imply that the additional labour 'put into motion' need also be productive labour. For such a possibility to be realized it is necessary that the 'revenue' received by the capitalist and by the landowner is transformed into capital or, to use Smith's expression, *accumulated*. And for Smith the accumulation of capital comes about, without exception, through advances of the means of production to extra productive labour: 'What is annually saved is as regularly consumed as what is annually spent, and nearly in the same time too; but it is consumed by a different set of people. That portion of his revenue which a rich man annually spends, is in most cases consumed by idle guests, and menial servants, who leave nothing behind them in return for their consumption. That portion which he annually saves, as for the sake of the profit it is immediately employed as a capital, is consumed in the same manner, and nearly in the same time too, but by a different set of people, by labourers, manufacturers, and artificers, who reproduce with a profit the value of their annual consumption. His revenue, we shall suppose, is paid him in money. Had he spent the whole, the food, clothing, and lodging which the whole could have purchased would have been distributed among the former set of people. By saving a part of it, so that part is for the sake of the profit immediately employed as a capital either by himself or by some other person, the food, clothing, and lodging, which may be purchased with it, are necessarily for the latter. The consumption is the same, but the consumers are different.'[16] Evidently the notion that all accumulated capital is resolved into the wages of additional labourers (and hence into the consumption of the latter) represents an analogous point of view with that implied in the idea sometimes adopted by Smith to the effect that value is directly made up of three types of income. The value component of the means of production in accumulated capital is ignored in the same way as it is not included as a component part of a commodity's value. Not until Marx do we find rigorous distinctions drawn between: (a) the total value of a good and the combined value of wages and surplus; (b) (following from (a)), the total value of social production and the value of incomes distributed during the period of production; and finally (c) aggregate accumulation and that part of the aggregate that consists of wage advances. However the fact that Smith resolves total accumulation into the wages of productive labour serves to highlight the way in which he looked at growth, especially when the term 'value' is taken to refer to the entire social product which Smith does almost all the time in this part of his work.

We can say, then, that Adam Smith saw the relationship between social product and the quantity of labour it can command as an exchange relationship; one to which he certainly attached a much greater significance than that appertaining to individual exchange rates between different goods because of its importance as a criterion of the performance of the economy. Thus, if the social product is the result of productive labour, and if the net product or surplus is expended in capital formation, then the quantitative relationship between social product and embodied labour measures the quantity of potential additional labour brought into the economic system, and as such is a measure of the success of the economic process.

Smith looks at such a measure of success in at least two different ways. First of all, the wage level, as he makes clear,[17] depends not on the absolute level of demand for labour, but on the rate of change of demand. Wages are higher the greater is the rate of increase in demand for labour, and since this rate of increase depends in turn upon the accumulation of capital, the level of wages is dependent on the rate of accumulation.

As wages constitute the income of by far the greater part of society, an increase in the wage rate, or natural price of labour, is an essential element of public prosperity. 'The liberal reward of labour, therefore, as it is the effect of increasing wealth, so it is the cause of increasing population. To complain of it, is to lament over the necessary effect and cause of the greatest public prosperity.'[18] We need to distinguish between two possible effects that accumulation might have on wages, both of which were discussed by Smith, though he did not always differentiate between them. The first relates to the short period in which Smith, echoing a widely accepted opinion of his time, held that a rise in wages above their natural level would stimulate a growth of population. This increase in labour supply would have the effect of lowering wages so that they once again accorded with the natural rate.[19] The other possibility is that the effects of accumulation on the wage level can be permanent, so that the natural price of labour itself is increased. 'As one mode of expense [resulting in the maintenance of productive labour] is more favourable than the other [which results in the maintenance of unproductive labour] to the opulence of the individual, so it is likewise to that of a nation. The houses, the furniture, the clothing of the rich, in a little time, become useful to the inferior and middling ranks of people. They are able to purchase them when their superiors grow weary of them, and the general accommodation of the whole people is thus generally improved, when this mode of expense becomes universal among men of fortune. What was formerly a seat of the family of Seymour, is now an inn upon the Bath road. The marriage-bed of James the First of Great Britain, which his Queen brought with her from Denmark, as a present for a sovereign to make to a sovereign, was, a few years ago, the ornament of an ale house at Dunfermline.'[20]

Apart from the long-term effects of accumulation on the natural price of labour, Smith also approved of accumulation because it brings about increased employment. The transformation of the surplus to a fund destined for the maintenance of productive labour, by systematically increasing the *labour commanded* value of society's annual product, allows the growing population to find employment. There is thus a growing paid work force, rather than an increase in the impoverished unemployed.

All these reasons explain Smith's well-known judgement: 'every prodigal appears to be a public enemy, and every frugal man a public benefactor'.[21] To appreciate properly the significance of Smith's analysis, one must consider the historical setting to which it referred. Society in Smith's time was changing from a feudal economy to a capitalistic/bourgeois economy, and we must take account of the significance of the part played by the capitalistic accumulation process in this change. The feudalistic type of economic organization was going through a crisis which arose from the production process being devoted to the consumption needs of the aristocracy. Now it is clear that, though such consumption may become large in the course of time, it must still be limited, in which case there is a likelihood that an increasing proportion of the natural increase in population will remain unemployed. This can be described in Smithian terms as follows: because the surplus accruing to a feudal society is almost entirely expended on unproductive workers, society is condemned to be stationary so that growth of employment and an increase in the workers' standard of life are either non-existent or negligible. The capitalist economy with its essential characteristic of accumulation thus appeared to Smith as essential to the solution of a profound historical crisis. Smith's fame lies in his historical awareness, and his recognition of the radical changes wrought by capitalistic organization on the old fabric of society. Associated with this is the decisive task to which political economy, with its realistic insights, can address itself in the analysis of the new society: 'Political economy, considered as a branch of the science of a statesman or legislator, proposes two distinct objects: first to provide a plentiful revenue or subsistence for the people, or more properly to enable them to provide such a revenue or subsistence for themselves; and secondly, to supply the state or commonwealth with a revenue sufficient for the public services. It proposes to enrich both the people and the sovereign.'[22]

We will now go on to deal briefly with particular problems arising from Smith's growth theory as outlined above, together with a discussion of the role of the state in the growth of the nation's wealth.

6

Our examination of Smith's value theory has shown how he derived the value of goods from the 'natural levels' of wages, profit, and rent. Though the inadequacy of his procedure has already been noted, we shall continue the discussion so as to clarify better what Smith meant by the respective 'natural levels' of the three types of income.

In a capitalistic economy, where wage consists of the product of labour after the deductions of rent and profits, Smith first of all makes clear that there is a minimum wage which the labourer must receive. This is because: 'a man must always live by his work, and his wages must at least be sufficient to maintain him. They must even upon most occasions be somewhat more; otherwise it would be impossible for him to bring up a family, and the race of such workmen could not last beyond the first generation.' [23] We are thus concerned with a level of subsistence and reproduction though, as we have seen, the calculation of this level includes not only physiological factors but customary elements too which relate to that gradual increase and changing composition of the bundle of goods the labourer deems necessary to his subsistence and reproduction. [24] In addition, Smith carefully describes the process by which the market wage rate systematically tends towards the minimum wage which then becomes the 'natural' wage, so that the two merge into one. The way in which this happens is, first through the relative bargaining strengths of the masters and workers, and secondly through population changes. On the first question Smith said: 'What are the common wages of labour depends everywhere upon the contract usually made between these two parties, whose interests are by no means the same. The workmen desire to get as much, the master to give as little as possible. The former are disposed to combine in order to raise, the latter in order to lower the wages of labour.' [25] Smith affirms that the masters are always destined to have the advantage because: (1) their small numbers make it easier for them to combine than the many workers; (2)

while laws authorize or, at least, do not prohibit combinations between the masters, they prohibit those between workers; (3) the masters can sustain the struggle much longer than can the workers: the former can live on their capitals for a year or two, whereas the greater part of the latter would find it difficult to subsist for more than a week.[26]

Even if disparity of bargaining conditions were not in itself sufficient systematically to sink wages to the minimum level, population changes would occur to produce the same effect. If the demand for labour 'is continually increasing, the reward of labour must necessarily encourage in such a manner the marriage and multiplication of labourers, as may enable them to supply that continually increasing demand by a continually increasing population. If the reward should at any time be less than what was requisite for this purpose, the deficiency of hands would soon raise it, and if at any time it should be more, their excessive multiplication would soon lower it to this necessary rate. The market would be so much under-stocked with labour in the one case, and so much over-stocked in the other, as would soon force back its price to that proper rate which the circumstances of the society required.'[27] We may thus sum up as follows: the greater bargaining power of the capitalist with respect to that of the worker, together with the population movements induced by any differences between the market wage rate and the 'natural' rate, will ensure a systematic tendency for wages to be at their 'natural level'. Though the 'natural' levels in progressive societies would still be minimum levels of subsistence and reproduction, there will be a long-term tendency for these levels to be raised and qualitatively improved. It may be noted that Smith does not comment on the essential difference between the bargaining and population mechanism, above all as regards the time period required by each before they become effective. The powerlessness of population changes as a means of resolving short-period divergences between the market wage and 'natural' wage will later be disclosed by Marx. Marx clearly parts from a long tradition in the history of thought on this question, in as much as he attempts to confine the wage regulation mechanism within the strictly economic field through his demonstration of the phenomenon of the 'industrial reserve army'.

In so far as profit is concerned, two aspects of Smith's thought will be considered. The first is that Smith thought the rate of interest to be the most important indicator of what the rate of profit would be in various circumstances of time and place: 'It may be laid down as a maxim, that wherever a great deal can be made by the use of money, a great deal will commonly be given for the use of it; and that whenever little can be made by it, less will commonly be given for it. According therefore, as the usual market rate of interest varies in any country, we may be assured that the ordinary profits of stock must vary with it, must sink as it sinks, and rise as it rises. The progress of interest, therefore, may lead us to form some notion of the progress of profit.'[28] The second is his supposition that the rate of profit (which can be deduced from changes in the rate of interest associated with the progress of society) will tend to fall with the accumulation of capital. In his opinion, just as accumulation is the basic reason for an increase in the 'natural' level of wages, so it is the root cause of the fall in the 'natural' rate of profit. Smith does not give an exhaustive explanation of why this should be so, confining himself to the statement that in the same way as a flow of capital into a particular line of business will lower the rate of profit in that line, so will the general rate of profit be lowered when there is an increase in capital in all branches of industry.[29] That this explanation cannot be satisfactory becomes clear when one bears in mind that the effect that an inflow of capital into a particular industry has on the rate of profit in that industry can hardly be generalized to the entire economic system. In this particular case the effect on profit is a result of the fall in the relative price of the industrial product concerned, and it is quite clear that there is no sense in talking of a relative lowering of all prices in the aggregate market. Despite the inadequacy of this explanation, Smith's thesis is still important from the point of view of the history of doctrine, since the problem formulated is one that reappears, in various guises, throughout the history of economic thought. We will see how Ricardo later takes up the question of the long-term fall in the profit rate.

Finally, we turn to rent, which Smith defines as 'the price paid for the use of land'[30] which the landlord is able to appropriate by virtue of the monopoly that land ownership confers on him.[31] In contrast to the wage case, where the 'natural' level is a minimum level, Smith views the 'natural' rent level as a maximum level. He does so in the sense that rent is comprised of the *total* value of agricultural produce that is in excess of the capital advanced by the tenant farmer together with the normal rate of profit prevailing in the economy.[32] It is therefore the case that rent is greater or less according to the degree of fertility of the land and also according to its situation *vis-à-vis* the market,[33] though some rent will be paid for any land whatever.[34] We can say, then, that Smith admitted the existence of a differential rent (in the same sense as later defined by Malthus and Ricardo), and of an absolute rent.

The admission of an absolute rent led Smith to the formulation of a thesis peculiar to him, *viz.*: labour in agriculture is more productive than all other forms of labour because, besides producing its own subsistence and profit, it also produces a rent.[35] In putting forward this point of view (which has physiocratic overtones) Smith is obliged to abandon the idea expressed earlier that rent is due to a monopoly since in that case rent cannot be attributed to the greater productivity of agriculture, but only the imperfect functioning of the competitive mechanism. He is therefore forced to resort to the physiocratic thesis that in agriculture, and only in agriculture, labour is assisted by the special productivity of the 'powers of nature'.[36] In so doing Smith breaks faith with his essential contribution with regard to physiocratic thought, which is that *nothing* is productive without labour. In effect, what emerges from the consideration of the 'spontaneous' productions of the earth is that in the determination of rent and other forms of income what matters is not physical productivity but value productivity. From this point of view two cases should be considered: either less fertile land is available in practically unlimited quantities (as Ricardo, for example, always assumed) in which case some of it pays no rent because the value of the produce is only just sufficient to replace the capital expended together with normal profit—and the question of whether agricultural labour is more productive than other kinds of labour does not even present itself; or, less fertile land is scarce so that its owner is able to obtain rent for its use, in which case according to Smith's first hypothesis rent is a monopoly payment arising out of scarcity and has nothing to do with supposed differences in productivity between different sectors.

The fourth book of the *Wealth of Nations* contains a detailed exposition of the Smithian thesis as to the advantages of economic freedom. It is especially interesting to note that Smith's position is completely devoid of overall plan, and in order to show this it will be sufficient here to give an account of what he says, in marked contrast with mercantilist theory, on restrictions on the importation of those foreign goods which could be produced at home (that is, his discussion in Chapter II, Book IV).

Smith begins by showing that trade restrictions brought about by high import duties or absolute prohibitions, in so far as they confer a monopoly on certain domestic industries, will result in a greater quantity of labour and capital investment in those industries than would otherwise have occurred. But this change in the nation's composition of economic organization is not deemed to be in the interest of society as a whole. In the first place, the total level of economic activity as measured by the level of employment is constrained by the nation's capital supply, and no provision of a commercial nature can alter the quantity of capital possessed by the nation; and secondly, every individual, in his desire to employ his capital in order to secure maximum profits, unknowingly distributes total capital between various employments in such a way as to maximize national income. Thus any provision that induces individuals to allocate their capital in a non-spontaneous way must lower national income. In this specific case import restrictions would lead individuals to invest in industries which, because foreign goods are cheaper, they would have avoided under free-trade conditions. National interest would have been better promoted if individuals had been allowed to invest freely since, through international trade, the same quantity of domestic capital would have given rise to a greater quantity of goods obtained. Thus no policy can, in general, be more effective in the promotion of national wealth than the working of the *invisible hand*. The stimulus of private advantage leads individuals to unknowingly promote an end—the welfare of society—that had no part in their intentions.[37]

Smith considers the objection that import restrictions are useful in so far as they sometimes allow a given domestic industry to grow more rapidly than it would have done otherwise. Thus, a commodity which is in fact advantageous to import because it is cheaper than producing it at home, could, after a given period, be produced at home under conditions no less, and perhaps more, favourable than those pertaining abroad. Smith opposed such a view by asserting that economic activity can increase only in proportion to the increase of national capital. Since capital can only increase in proportion to an increase in savings, and since savings in turn can only increase with revenue, then it is extremely unlikely that such a provision, the immediate effect of which is to lower income, can lead to a greater increase in capital than would have naturally taken place.[38]

Smith does, however, recognize at least two situations which admit import restriction. The first concerns the protection of an industry essential to national defence: 'The defence of Great Britain, for example, depends very much upon the number of its sailors and shipping. The act of navigation, therefore, very properly endeavours to give the sailors and shipping of Great Britain the monopoly of the trade of their own country, in some cases, by absolute prohibitions, and in others by heavy burdens upon the shipping of foreign countries.'[39] Such an act is thus acceptable, even though it is 'not favourable to foreign commerce, or to the growth of that opulence which can arise from it'. The second case in which it is opportune to restrict imports is where there exists a domestic levy on a home produced good. In such circumstances, the imposition of an equal tax on the same product produced abroad will not result in the creation of a domestic monopoly, but will simply restore parity between the home produced and foreign commodity.[40]

Just as there are two circumstances in which import restrictions must be considered opportune, so there are two further occasions where restrictions are a matter for debate.

The first deals with deciding upon the extent to which a nation may follow a policy of reprisal against a foreign country that discriminates against its imports. In Smith's opinion a policy of reprisal only makes sense in so far as there is some probability that it will result in the cessation of foreign restriction, so that general freedom of trade will ensue. When no such probability exists reprisal is noxious because it aggravates the situation which has already been provoked by the mistaken policy of others.[41]

The second case concerns the timing and degree of restoration of free importation when trade has been interrupted for some period of time. The problem is that some manufacturers that have developed because of trade restrictions, will be in serious difficulties when free trade is resumed. The greatest sufferers would certainly be the workmen who have found employment in these trades. Smith's opinion is that in such circumstances one must employ a certain prudence in the return to free trade, but that the inherent difficulties should not be exaggerated. After all, there is in general little difficulty in absorbing large numbers of workmen into civilian occupations as has been evidenced by the demobilization of soldiers at the end of a war. Similarly, there cannot be serious impediments to the gradual reabsorption into alternative employment of workers who find themselves unemployed as a result of some industries being hit by the freeing of trade.[42]

Smith's treatment of *laissez-faire* portrays most of the problems subsequently tackled in economic thought. The following two observations will suffice here. The first concerns the justification behind the case for free trade. The justification offered by Smith—that importation is advantageous whenever a commodity is produced more cheaply abroad than at home—necessarily leads to the absurdity that a country which produces all commodities at higher costs than those of others must import all commodities without producing any itself. As indicated, this problem will be resolved by Ricardo's demonstration that free trade is beneficial whenever there is a divergence between comparative costs rather than absolute costs. That is, a country that has an absolute disadvantage in all manufactures will none the less benefit through concentrating its production in those lines where the disadvantage is relatively less. The second observation refers to the infant industry argument, which supposes commercial protection such that a domestic industry protected from international competition will eventually become sufficiently established to stand on its own. It is clear that Smith's arguments against such a policy are inconclusive. The fact that protection results in a short-period diminution of income does not imply that long-term advantages gained cannot be great enough to overcome initial losses. More recent economic thought has recognized that commodity costs between different countries depend not only on initial endowments of natural resources but also on the quantity and types of capitals possessed by any particular country. In other words, since international cost structures depend not only upon different natural endowments of resources but also on the different amounts and kinds of capital accumulated by different countries, and especially, on historical factors, it need not follow that initial cost structures be accepted as non-changeable data. Indeed, free international trade tends to perpetuate the initial situation and so can positively hinder some countries' potential development—we need only to look at the division between industrial and agricultural countries (and hence, in substance, to the separation between developed and underdeveloped countries), which raises the question of the justification for accepting such division as the basis for the international division of labour.

There is no doubt, however, that for the situation Smith had in mind (where all the countries concerned were, in various degrees, already developed, such as Great Britain, Holland, and France) the free trade thesis represented a decisive scientific contribution to the end of promoting general wealth. It must also be remembered that Smith did not have much hope that his recommendations, which to him appeared and in fact were consonant with national economic development, would be calmly accepted. He thought that his proposals would be opposed by special interests, in particular by the merchants and capitalists who were ever seeking monopoly positions and ever disposed to exercise all possible political pressure to obtain them.[43]

8

More than a quarter of the *Wealth of Nations* is devoted to the examination of the expenses and revenue sources of the sovereign or commonwealth. Here it is only possible to outline very briefly Smith's work in this field, with the sole purpose of giving some idea of how he conceived the functions of the state in the economic system.

Smith has a threefold classification of public expenses: the expense of defence; the expense of the administration of justice; and the expense of public works and public institutions. The latter category includes firstly the expense of the construction of works intended to facilitate commerce (roads, ports, navigable canals, bridges, etc., including fortifications necessary to defend trading stations established in primitive countries); secondly, expenses incurred in the education of youth and in the religious instruction of people of all ages; and thirdly, expenses necessary to support the dignity of the sovereign. The basic principle justifying public works is made quite clear by Smith in the following statement: 'though they [public works and institutions] may be in the highest degree advantageous to a great society, they are, however, of such a nature, that the profit could never repay the expense to any individual or small number of individuals, and which it therefore cannot be expected that any individual or small number of individuals should erect or maintain'.[44]

Smith is interesting on the way in which different state expenditures should be met, especially on the question of whether the tax burden should be collectively shared or whether it should be met only by the direct beneficiaries of state services. The expense of defence and the maintenance of the dignity of the sovereign must be indifferently borne by all, for all derive benefit from such expense in equal measure. The expense of justice must in part be met by the public as a whole given that the administration of justice, either directly or indirectly, is to everybody's advantage. But in part it is better met by those who have occasion for the exercise of justice, either by transgression of the law or indeed its use for the restoration or protection of their rights. Public works are beneficial to the community as a whole and hence the community, at least in part, should finance them. But in part they should be financed by the more direct gainers whose commercial activities depend more on the public services. The same kind of thing holds for the expense of education for the young and for religious instruction. Such expenditures are certainly to the benefit of the entire community and as such can be financed by all. But they may also in part be financed by the direct gainers, with some advantage, according to Smith, in education, since a teacher who draws his income not only from a fixed stipend but also from his pupils' contributions is especially stimulated to earn for himself, through the excellence of his teaching and assiduity, the gratitude and consideration of those whom he teaches.[45]

As regards the sources of state revenue Smith distinguishes between revenue from state-owned property and revenue from taxation. The former source he judged unsuitable and too small to bear the public expenditure of a great and civilized state. Public expenditure must therefore be mainly met through taxation.[46] For this purpose Smith enunciates his four famous maxims: (1) 'The subjects of every state ought to contribute towards the support of the government, as nearly as possible, in proportion to their respective abilities; that is, in proportion to the revenue which they respectively enjoy under the protection of the state'; (2) 'The tax which each individual is bound to pay ought to be certain, and not arbitrary. The time of payment, the manner of payment, the quantity to be paid, ought to be clear and plain to the contributor, and to every other person'; (3) 'Every tax ought to be levied at the time, or in the manner in which it is most likely to be convenient, for the contributor to pay it'; (4) 'Every tax ought to be so contrived as both to take and to keep out of the pockets of the people as little as possible over and above what it brings into the public treasury of the state.'[47]

Bearing in mind that the private income of citizens is made up of rent, profit, and wages any tax must by definition be paid by some combination of these three income sources. Smith accordingly distinguishes four types of taxes: those intended to bear on rent; those intended for profit; those intended to bear on wages; and, finally, taxes which bear indifferently on all the three income sources.[48] A tax on rent is the one most preferred because it least disturbs the formation of wealth: 'Both ground-rents and the ordinary rent of land are a species of revenue which the owner, in many cases, enjoys without any care or attention of his own. Though a part of this revenue should be taken from him in order to defray the expenses of the state, no discouragement will thereby be given to any sort of industry. The annual produce of the land and labour of the society, the real wealth and revenue of the great body of the people, might be the same after such a tax as before. Ground-rents, and the ordinary rent of land, are, therefore, perhaps, the species of revenue which can best bear to have a peculiar tax imposed upon them.'[49]

To evaluate the effect of a tax on profit we need to distinguish the pure interest on capital component of profits from the reward for risking the capital stock in the employment concerned. A tax on gross profit (assuming that it can be evaluated, which Smith thinks very unlikely) can only have two effects. Either prices are increased to cover the tax, in which case the tax is transferred to those who buy the goods produced by the capital, or prices are not increased, in which case the tax must then have the effect of reducing the pure capital interest element of profits, because that part of profit relating to risk incurred is the minimum acceptable to the capitalists if they are to invest. But a fall in the interest received would bring about a transfer of domestic capital abroad, because 'The proprietor of stock is properly a citizen of the world, and is not necessarily attached to any particular country.' [50] Thus, a tax on profit, for these reasons, is much less opportune than a tax on rent, either because the tax will not really be met out of profits or because a tax which reduces profits will lead to a falling off of the country's economic activity. [51]

Where a tax on wages is concerned it is pointed out that as the 'natural' wage level is a minimum level, it is impossible for the tax to be really paid out of wages. It is therefore passed on and always falls on profit, so that a tax on wages follows the same rules as a tax on profits. In particular a wage tax will very probably lead to a fall in the demand for labour and hence to a decline in economic activity. 'The declension of industry, the decrease of employment for the poor, the diminution of the annual produce of the land and labour of the country, have generally been the effects of such taxes.' [52]

Finally, taxes that are intended to fall indifferently on all types of income are capitation taxes and (indirect) taxes on goods. Capitation taxes, if taken to be proportionate to the fortune or to the income of each contributor, are necessarily arbitrary because 'The state of a man's fortune varies from day to day, and without an inquisition more intolerable than any tax, and renewed at least once a year, can only be guessed at.' If instead the taxes are 'proportioned not to the supposed fortune, but to the rank of each contributor [they] become altogether unequal; the degrees of fortune being frequently unequal in the same degree of rank'. Such taxes are therefore to be avoided, since 'if it is attempted to render them equal, [they] become altogether arbitrary and uncertain; and if it is attempted to render them certain and not arbitrary, [they] become altogether unequal'.[53] Indirect taxes, if they are imposed on basic necessities, present the same inconveniences as a tax on wages. But they are acceptable when they are imposed on luxury goods, because they then fall mainly on rent.[54]

The conclusion of Smith's inquiry is that taxes, whether direct or indirect, should mainly fall on rent. And it is clear that such a conclusion is the most reasonable taxation thesis when one deals, as Smith implicitly does, with a society in which 'natural' wage is a subsistence and reproduction minimum and in which profit is mainly devoted to capital formation.

9

If one considers Smith's thought in its entirety, it is difficult to escape the impression that, basically, no problem is resolved by him in a satisfactory manner. His analysis of value theory involves him in a considerable logical difficulty. His conceptual determination of national income is faulty because of his identification of income with the value of production. His identification of wage advances with capital formation is unsatisfactory as is his analysis of the fall in the rate of profit which extends considerations pertinent only to a single industry to the entire economy. His rent analysis is marred by the lack of clarity as to the origin of absolute rent, and finally his espousal of economic liberty must appear today to involve a simplistic identification of private with social interest.

The real significance of this great thinker lies in his formulation, through a unique structure of thought, of nearly all the problems that were later taken up by further scientific thought, and especially important is his striking and nearly complete comprehension of the special nature of the new economic order that came into being with the emergence of the bourgeoisie. The bourgeoisie are properly recognized for the first time in Smith's work, as 'citizens of the world' who bring together different nations in their systematic pursuit of economic expansion. In this sense the tradition that regards Smith as the father of political economy takes on an undoubted truth. Smith is the point of departure for all later lines of inquiry, and later economists are measured by their response to questions he initially set.

References

1. *An Inquiry into the Nature and Causes of the Wealth of Nations.* The standard edition is that of E. Cannan of 1904.

2. *Lectures on Justice, Police, Revenue and Arms, delivered in the University of Glasgow by Adam Smith, reported by a student in 1763,* edited by E. Cannan (Oxford, 1896); this edition has been reprinted by A. M. Kelley (New York, 1964).

3. *Glasgow Lectures*, p. 176.

4. Op. cit., p. 15.

5. *Glasgow Lectures*, p. 171.

6. In fact one at times comes across a physiocratic residuum in Smith, based on the assumption that labour employed on land is more productive than that employed elsewhere (see, e.g., *Wealth of Nations*, I, pp. 343–4). We shall examine the reason for the persistence of this notion in Smith when we come to consider his theory of rent.

7. *Wealth of Nations*, I, p. 50

8. Ibid., I, p. 67.

9. Ibid., I, pp. 67–8.

10. Ibid., I, p. 88.

11. Ibid., pp. 32–3.

12. Ibid., pp. 49–50.

13. Ibid., I, p. 52.

14. Ibid., I, p. 51.

15. Ibid., I, p. 67.

16. Ibid., I, pp. 320–1.

17. Ibid., I, pp. 70–5.

18. Ibid., I, p. 83.

19. Ibid., I, p. 83.

20. Ibid., I, p. 329.

21. Ibid., I, p. 323

22. Ibid., I, p. 395.

23. Ibid., I, pp. 69–70.

24. Ibid., I, p. 80.

25. Ibid., I, p. 68.

26. Ibid., I, p. 68.

27. Ibid., I, pp. 81–2.

28. Ibid., I, p. 90.

29. Ibid., I, p. 89.
30. Ibid., I, p. 145.
31. *Wealth of Nations*, I, p. 146.
32. Ibid., I, p. 146.
33. Ibid., I, p. 148.
34. Ibid., I, p. 147. Smith also considers the case where no rent is paid for the use of land (See I, p. 162 *et seq.*); but such a case, in his opinion, is only true in special circumstances appertaining to particular products e.g. raw materials for manufactures.
35. Ibid., I, pp. 343–4.
36. Ibid., I, p. 344.
37. Ibid., I, p. 419.
38. Ibid., I, p. 423.
39. Ibid., I, p. 427.
40. Ibid., I, p. 429.
41. Ibid., I, p. 432. Smith asserts that 'To judge whether such retaliations are likely to produce such an effect, does not, perhaps, belong so much to the science of a legislator . . . as to the skill of that insidious and crafty animal, vulgarly called a statesman or politician.'
42. Ibid., I, pp. 434–435.
43. Ibid., I, p. 435.
44. Ibid., II, p. 214.
45. Ibid., II, p. 299, and in particular on the expense of education see II, pp. 249–50 and II, p. 255.
46. Ibid., II, p. 309.
47. Ibid., II, pp. 310–11.
48. Ibid., II, p. 310.
49. Ibid., II, p. 328.
50. Ibid., II, p. 333.
51. Ibid., II, p. 333.
52. Ibid., II, p. 350.
53. Ibid., II, p. 352.
54. Ibid., II, p. 370.

Four:

Ricardo

While Smith had defined economics as the science of the wealth of nations, or as the science that is concerned with the ways in which the wealth of 'the sovereign or commonwealth' will be maximized, Ricardo defines political economy as that science which is concerned with the distribution of the social product between the various classes of society. Or, to be more precise, Ricardo judged economics to deal with the distribution of social product between wages, profit, and rent.[1]

The reason for allotting this role to economic science is that, by so doing, Ricardo succeeds in investing the science with a fully operational recognition of the capitalistic character of the economy. This typical characteristic of his thought enabled him to make a net advance over Smith's contribution.

We will recall that though Smith did in fact realize more fully than the Physiocrats the capitalistic nature of the economy, various aspects of his work were not always in accordance with his overall vision. This is because various aspects of his work, and especially many of his examples, refer to economic subjects which relate not to a capitalistic society, but a simple mercantilist society in which independent producers freely associate in the market place.

The point is that these mercantilistic relics (with one qualification dealt with below) completely disappear with Ricardo. The society he considers is completely capitalistic, and as such is divided into the three social classes of labourers, capital owners, and landowners. This tripartite class division of society was held by Ricardo to influence the development of economic life in such a way that it would be impossible scientifically to inquire into such development without taking as a point of departure the consideration of how these three classes share in the social product.

But before specifying the significance that Ricardo attached to the problem of distribution, one may bear in mind not so much the definition of the object of economic science that Ricardo gave at the beginning of his work, as the content of the later developments. Each one of the shares of national product has a determinate relationship with the 'resources' possessed by the corresponding social class. Thus that part which goes to wages has a given relationship with total labour employed, giving rise to a particular wage unit, or wage rate; the share of national product attributed to rent bears a specific relationship to the quantity of land engaged in the productive process, though, as we shall see, in this case one cannot properly speak of a rent unit; and, finally, the profit share is specifically related to the total capital involved, which determines the rate of profit.

The aspect of distribution Ricardo held to be most important was the determination of the value and progress of the rate of profit, especially as it bears on the wage rate.

There is no doubt that a striking confirmation of Ricardo's complete awareness of the nature of the capitalist economy is provided by his decision to place the problem of the rate of profit at the centre of economic theory, and to consider the distribution of the social product (net of rent) between capitalists and wage earners as a problem of the relationship between profit rate and wage rate rather than a problem of the determination of the relative shares of wages and profit in the national product. It is obvious, in fact, that the profit rate is the most fundamental economic factor in such an economy, since it absolutely determines the course and historical destiny of the capitalistic process.

2

The question of profit was tackled by Ricardo in two successive phases: the first is presented in his *Essay on Profits*[2] of 1815; the other in the three editions of the *Principles* that came out between

1817 and 1821. In the *Essay* of 1815 the examination of the determination and change of the rate of profit is based on the assumption that this question is inseparable from that of the determination
and change of agricultural rent. Ricardo's fundamental idea is that
the course of the economy's general profit rate depends upon the
rate of profit earned in agriculture, and that an examination of the
latter is at the same time an examination of agricultural rent.[3]

The rent question is determined by Ricardo on a basis that had
already in part been established by Smith but later more fully
developed by Anderson, West, and Malthus. These authors'
contributions enabled the process that gives rise to differential rent
to be posed in the following terms: at the beginning of a given
process of national development, one may suppose that current
food requirements would be met by cultivating only the more
fertile and better located lands. In this first phase, in which the
type of land put under cultivation is available in almost unlimited
quantities, rent does not exist, and the product drawn from a given
piece of land, net of all costs, is fully converted into the profit of
the capitalist who has invested his capital in the land. In Ricardo's
example one would obtain, from the better land, 300 quarters of
wheat from an annual capital advance (including wages) that has a
value equivalent of 200 quarters, and the rate of profit is as 1 : 2,
that is 50 per cent. If, after a process of development, one must
bring less fertile and/or less favourably situated land into cultivation, one will (say) obtain from them an average product of 300
quarters of wheat only if one makes a larger capital advance, say
210 quarters. In that case the rate of profit on the less fertile land
will be as 90 : 210, or 43 per cent. On the other hand, because of
the effect of competition, the land cultivated during the first phase
cannot earn a rate of profit greater than that earned on the marginal
land. This implies that, of the net 'first phase' product of 100
quarters, only 86 quarters (equal to 43 per cent of 200) will be
collected as profit, while the remaining 14 quarters will form the
landlord's rent. Thus, the cultivation of land during the second
phase gives rise to a *differential* rent on land cultivated in the first
phase. Continuing the process, a third area of land even less fertile
or more distant from the market will be brought under cultivation.
On this land an investment equivalent to 220 quarters (say) will
be required to raise 300 quarters of wheat, and the resulting 80

quarters of net product give rise to a profit of 36 per cent. Such a rate of profit applied to the capital invested on the former land will produce a profit of 72 quarters on the first type, and hence a rent of 28, and a profit of 76 quarters on the second type of land and hence a rent of 14. So the process gradually goes on, and the rate of profit falls. It is significant that, at least after a certain limit, the amount of profit also falls, while rent increases either because new land, from time to time, gives rise to a differential rent, or because the rent on land already utilized increases.

Agricultural profit rate determines the general rate of profit because competition equalizes the profit rates between different sectors, and since the tendency for a falling agricultural profit rate must be transmitted to the general rate of profit, the latter must also manifest a tendency to decrease.

However, some problems arise here which, it may be said, Ricardo had already alluded to within the structure of the *Essay*. His final deliberation on these was made immediately after the publication of the *Essay*; and the results he reached are to be found in the *Principles* of 1817 which, though it was initiated as an amplification of the 1815 *Essay*, was transformed by virtue of these problems into an entirely new work.

The fundamental question which arose may be put in the following way: when Ricardo determined the course of the rate of profit as a function of the extension of cultivation, he reduced all the capital advanced in agricultural production into quarters of wheat. Thus, for example, the 200 quarters of wheat invested on a portion of land of the first type was in part directly made up of wheat in the form of wage advances, but was also in part made up of other means of production expressed in quarters of wheat on the basis of their prices and the price of corn. Therefore the Ricardian calculation, and the conclusions derived from it, came to depend on the assumption that the prices of means of production remain constant and are independent of the process studied by Ricardo, that is, the extension of cultivation to increasingly less productive land. On the other hand, it can be seen that this assumption is inadmissible, as Ricardo himself realized. He emphasized that the extension of cultivation to less productive land brought about an increase in the price of wheat relative to the prices of other goods, because the latter are unlikely to experience a parallel increase in the 'difficulties of production'.[4] This variation in the relative price of corn acts favourably on rent since, being paid in corn, it will be able to purchase more with the increase in corn price. But it also acts favourably on the profit rate since, as an agricultural profit is a corn profit while capital is only partly made up of corn, the ratio between profit and capital will rise when the price of corn rises with respect to the prices of the other means of production. It is therefore necessary to take account of the fact that in the development process described by Ricardo, while the acquisition of a given quantity of agricultural produce requires an increase of capital in a physical sense, that is, an increase in the quantity of the means of production advanced (which has an unfavourable effect on the rate of profit), the price of some part of these means of production will fall with respect to the product price (which will have a favourable effect on the profit rate). In these circumstances, the tendency of profit to fall can be demonstrated only when what happens in industry is also accounted for. As regards the latter, the increase in the price of corn, and therefore in the cost of capital advances as wages, is not compensated by an increase in product price. Therefore, the industrial rate of profit will fall, so, through the working of competition, causing the agricultural profit rate to fall. But this implies that the profit rate in industry determines that in agriculture, and not vice versa.[5]

Moreover, once the possibility, let alone necessity, that there will be changes in the relative price of corn compared with other goods is admitted, we need to take a further consideration into account. Ricardo admits in the *Essay* that better techniques can oppose the tendency for the rate of profit to fall. He did not attach decisive importance to this factor since he considered the influence exercised by it would not be sufficient to overcome the negative influence of the reduction of fertility. But if one admits that the underlying factors behind the exchange rate between corn and other goods are not constant, then another circumstance will come to have an influence on the agricultural profit rate, *viz.*: the improving techniques arising in sectors that directly or indirectly furnish the means of production in agriculture. Such improvements would in fact lower yet further the value of capital invested in agriculture with respect to the value of the agricultural product. Evidently, then, if the influence of technical progress is to be evaluated, taking into account not only technical progress in agriculture but also that in industry, the thesis that technical progress does not succeed in preventing the fall of the rate of profit becomes much less certain. However, in evaluating this influence one is again faced by the fact that the rate of agricultural profit is influenced by changes in the rate of profit of other sectors, and not vice versa.

This collection of questions was certainly what induced Ricardo, immediately after the publication of the *Essay*, to concentrate his attention on the problem of price. In a letter to James Mill written towards the end of 1815, when he had started to write the *Principles*, he said 'I know I shall be soon stopped by the word price.'[6]

3

We have yet to mention that the thesis of the dominant role of agricultural profit could have enabled a strict and unassailable formulation of a line of thought that appears to have been in Ricardo's mind,[7] based on the hypothesis that it is not too far removed from reality to assume that agricultural capital (wages advanced to the labourers), as well as the product, consists of corn only. If this is true, then the profit rate in agriculture can be determined in purely physical terms. An analogous though less rigid hypothesis was adopted, as we know, by the Physiocrats in their supposition that the means of production in agriculture are composed of the same goods as the product. And in effect the idea that Ricardo appears to have taken into consideration (which is, we repeat, that corn is the only commodity that makes up both capital and product) may be considered as taking the physiocratic supposition to its limits. However this simplifying hypothesis was never explicitly put forward by Ricardo; that he could have thought of it is mainly deduced from a letter written to him by Malthus on 5 August 1814, in which, objecting to a point of view that Ricardo must have expressed orally, he wrote: 'In no case of production is the produce exactly of the same nature as the capital advanced. Consequently we can never properly refer to a material rate of produce.'[8] But perhaps the more convincing proof that Ricardo was directing his thought in the direction discussed is in the kind of value theory he formulates in the *Principles*, since, as we shall see, this theory has a fundamental characteristic that permits the rate of profit to be determined in physical terms.

Before turning to this question, however, it would be useful to inquire a little more deeply as to how Ricardian theory would have developed if the corn hypothesis had been made completely explicit. It is clear, first of all, that in such a case the thesis that the agricultural profit rate determines the general rate of profit could have been very easily demonstrated. In fact, since the rate of profit in agriculture is determined in purely physical terms (that is, quite independently of the price system), the rate of profit in other sectors, through changes between the prices of goods with respect to corn by virtue of the competitive mechanism, would come to equal the agricultural profit rate. Moreover, the thesis of the fall of the rate of profit in agriculture (when one ignores possible improvements in corn production) can be established with great facility. If, in fact, to obtain a given increase in the quantity of corn over time, one must increase the quantity of corn advanced for the subsistence of labour, it immediately follows that the rate of profit falls.

It is worth while to elaborate this point in a little more detail. Let us suppose that annual corn production is obtained through the annual advance of corn, in such a way therefore that the annual cost of production has the same value as capital advanced. In this case the rate of profit is evidently worked out by taking the difference between annual corn produced and the corn employed as means of production during the year, and dividing this difference by the corn advanced. To be exact, this kind of calculation should be undertaken for marginal land, that is land for which according to Ricardo no rent is paid (as we have previously seen). For intra-marginal land, after having deducted annual cost in corn from annual production, one obtains a total that includes profit and rent and, having determined the profit on the basis of the rate of profit obtained on the marginal land, one obtains a final rent residual.

Thus, let x be the quantity of grain produced on the marginal land, L the quantity of labour employed on the land, with $a = x/L$ the quantity of corn produced by a labour unit on this land (which is the productivity of labour), and w the quantity of corn that corresponds to the wage rate. Since no rent is paid on the marginal land, profit is $x - wL$, and the rate of profit r is:

$$r = \frac{x - wL}{wL} = \frac{a}{w} - 1$$

Since one assumes that w is a constant at a level of subsistence and a is a decreasing function of employment (given that the productivity of labour falls gradually as the marginal lands become less fertile), r decreases as a function of employment (and hence with the extension of cultivation); and when a has finally fallen to the point of becoming equal to w (when, that is, all the product of the marginal land is absorbed by wages), the rate of profit is zero.

On each of the intra-marginal lands, the rent unit (that is, rent per labour unit) is given by the difference between the quantity of corn produced by a unit of labour on the land considered and the quantity of corn produced by a unit of labour on the marginal land. Total rent is obviously given by the product of unit rent and the quantity of labour employed on the land in question. In fact, if L^1 is the quantity of labour on an intra-marginal piece of land and a^1 is the quantity of corn produced on this land by a unit of labour, then wages on this land are wL^1 and the profit (calculated by applying the general rate of profit to the capital wL^1) is $rwL^1 = (a/w - 1)wL^1 = (a - w)L^1$. Rent, which is what remains of the product a^1L^1 after having deducted wages and profit is: $a^1L^1 - (a - w)L^1 - wL^1 = (a^1 - a)L^1$.

Considering agricultural production as a whole, one can see that with the increase in total production as a function of employment (1) total rent increases either because as a decreases the expression $(a^1 - a)$ becomes larger, or because previously marginal land becomes intra-marginal and receives a rent for the first time; (2) total wages increase because employment increases at a constant wage rate; (3) total profits, at least after a certain point, diminish because the tendency for r to fall to zero more than compensates for the increase in capital.

Naturally, as has been mentioned, the tendency for the agricultural profit rate to fall brings about an identical fall in the system as a whole, and the lowest limit of the profit level not only relates to agriculture but to the entire economy.

We repeat, however, that this idea of a technical identity of capital and product in agriculture was never developed by Ricardo. Indeed, the second phase of his thought as put forward in the *Principles*[9] begins with the full realization that—given the untenability of the unique hypothesis that the rate of profit can be given in purely physical terms, thus strictly justifying the thesis that agricultural profit rate regulates the general profit rate—the formulation of a theory of value is a prerequisite for the study of the determination and change of the rate of profit. Thus, the theory of value is in fact the first subject taken up in the *Principles*.

4

Ricardo elaborated his theory of value within the Smithian theoretic structure. We will recall that in Smith's theory of value, the exchange values of goods are made to depend on given quantities of labour, those quantities in fact that the various goods can 'put into motion' or 'command'. Ricardo could not fully accept the Smithian position, since he perceived that the quantity of labour that any single good can 'put into motion' requires the previous determination of the exchange rate between that good and labour. Thus, the ratio of exchange, which is what we wish to determine, has already been assumed in the valuation procedure, with an obvious circularity of argument.[10]

There was, however, an aspect of Smith's theory that Ricardo considered usable for the formulation of a correct theory of value. Smith had affirmed that in a pre-capitalist economy (and in this regard Smith had a simple mercantilist economy in mind), the quantity of labour put into motion by a given good is identified with the quantity of labour embodied in that good; whence the ratio of exchange between two goods becomes identical with the ratio between the quantities of labour embodied in the same goods.[11] Smith, as we have seen, held that this circumstance could not be held valid for a capitalistic economy. *The position of Ricardo is that, on the contrary, the fact that in a capitalistic economy a part of the product does not accrue to labour, because it is transformed into either profit or rent, does not in fact prevent the exchange of goods according to the quantity of labour embodied in them.*[12]

The better to understand Ricardo's criticism, it is advisable to recall Smith's argument. In the first place, if value is defined as labour commanded, then there is no doubt that labour embodied can only be taken into consideration in so far as it constitutes, in its turn, an explanation of labour commanded. And Smith had reason to state that this condition would certainly be true in a simple mercantilist economy. In fact, in such an economy, the quantity of labour purchased by a good, A, must be equal to the quantity of labour embodied in each of the goods with which A exchanges; and in that case the quantity of labour commanded by A is equal to the quantity of labour embodied in A. In a capitalist economy, things become complicated because, in the first place, the expression 'labour commanded' ceases to have an unequivocal meaning. In fact good A, when taken to a capitalistic market, can purchase labour in two senses: (1) because of the labour in the goods bought by A; (2) because A exchanges directly (by way of money) with labour. These two measures of labour commanded are not equal. The first, for the same reasons that apply in a simple mercantilist economy, is equal to the labour embodied in A. The second is greater than A's labour embodied: thus, suppose that there are 100 hours of labour embodied in a good, which are supplied by labourers whose subsistence cost 50 hours of labour; then this good can furnish the subsistence for a number of labourers capable of providing 200 hours of labour. In this case the labour embodied is 100 and the labour commanded is 200. Smith always refers to labour commanded in this second sense which, as we have noted, is different to the significance he attributed to labour commanded when he talks about a pre-capitalistic economy. Therefore the labour embodied in a good seems to him to be less than the labour commanded by the same good, and, since he found no way to explain the latter by the former, he had to abandon the labour embodied concept as an explanatory category of exchange value. Now, Ricardo's position can be interpreted as a call for consistency: if by labour commanded by a given good one *always* means the labour embodied in the goods for which it exchanges, if, that is, one holds constant the definition of labour embodied whether for a pre-capitalistic or a capitalistic economy, then the situation remains unchanged when passing from one economy to another. And if one can say that the ratio of exchange is equal to the ratio of labour embodied in a pre-capitalistic economy it can equally well be said for a capitalistic economy.

5

Before going on to Ricardo's statement it is useful to interpose a fuller appreciation of the sense and significance of Ricardo's response to Smith. This is because though Ricardo's criticism represented from one point of view a decisive advance over Smith in the development of value theory, on the other hand it involved the demise of Smith's basic *labour commanded* idea. The singling out of the negative and positive aspects of the Ricardian position (always remaining within labour value theory) cannot be properly carried out without recourse to some ideas introduced by Marx (who, as one would expect, was the first and only thinker to give an exact judgement on the relative merits and demerits of the value theories of Smith and Ricardo). It is thus necessary to begin with these Marxist ideas.

Let us take up again the distinction made a little earlier between the two ways in which one can arrive at the exchange between goods and labour in a capitalistic economy, and hence between the two meanings that 'labour commanded' can assume. In particular, let us dwell here on the second of the two alternative descriptions, that is on the direct exchange between goods and labour. In this exchange, as Marx will make clear, the good takes on a particular form in so far as one of the conditions of this exchange is that it becomes capital. Thus, one is really dealing with the exchange between capital and labour. Now, according to Marx (or, rather, according to the more rigorous formulation of the theory of labour value) this exchange possesses special characteristics that are not to be found in the general exchange of good against good. That is, one can begin by clearly reflecting on the fact that, despite appearances, one does not directly exchange capital with labour, for the good reason that labour is not like a commodity, nor can it be, given that it is the origin of the value of goods themselves. What capital directly exchanges against is in reality labour-power, or rather all the qualities possessed by the worker that makes him capable of giving labour. Labour-power is a commodity with the same status as any other whatsoever, and like others possesses a value given by the value necessary to produce it, that is by the labour that is necessary to produce the means of subsistence of the wage earner. The exchange between capital and labour is hence, in the first place, the same as an exchange of good against good, since one is dealing with the fact that goods which constitute capital are exchanged against a particular good—i.e. labour-power. On the other hand, once this exchange has taken place the purchaser of the labour-power, that is the capitalist, like any other buyer of whatever goods, can draw from it its use value, which in the specific case of labour-power is, in fact, the labour that labour-power can give to the productive process. In this sense one can also say that the capital exchanged for labour, or more properly, by means of the exchange between capital and labour-power (which is exchange in the proper rather than analogical sense) the same capital has under its control (or, to use Smith's expression, 'command') a given quantity of labour. The Marxian distinction between labour and labour-power very readily permits the determination of the surplus, the common origin of profit and rent. Since the quantity of labour that the worker renders to the productive process is greater (in a measure dependent on labour productivity) than the quantity of labour embodied in labour-power, there is a difference between labour rendered and that part of it corresponding to the reconstitution of the value of labour-power. Thus, the labour surplus that is ever present in the production process necessarily gives rise to a surplus value from which is drawn both profit and rent. In other words, total labour rendered is always made up of two parts: necessary labour that reproduces the value of labour-power, and surplus labour that produces surplus value. Thus, the sense in which Marx says that necessary labour is paid labour, while surplus labour is unpaid labour, is made clear.

Having said all this, let us see how one can re-interpret the Ricardian criticism of Smith, and in this way establish the merits and demerits of the two positions. To facilitate the discussion we refer to the following example. Consider a good which requires, for its production, 100 hours of labour, of which 80 hours represent necessary labour and 20 represent surplus labour. If this good is exchanged against labour-power, it will exchange for a quantity of labour-power that has a value corresponding to 100 hours of labour. The exchange in question will be in full accordance with the law of labour value. On the other hand the labour-power purchased will be able to provide a quantity of labour equal to 100:0·8; or 125 hours of labour. Faced with this situation Smith would reason thus: A good that contains labour equal to 100 commands a quantity equal to 125. The two quantities of labour do not coincide and hence labour embodied cannot be assumed to explain exchange value. Ricardo's objection may then be put in the following way: the quantity of labour embodied cannot be compared with the quantity of 'living labour' that this commodity, as capital, will be able to command, because in that way one comes to speak not of real exchange, but of an exchange that is such only be analogy. Real exchange is that between capital and labour-power and, in this exchange one has an equality between the labour embodied in the good, i.e. in the capital, and the quantity embodied in labour power. There is a full application, therefore, of the labour embodied principle.

Marx's judgement of the two positions is as follows: there is a sense in which Ricardo's criticism of Smith is correct, because when one tests the proposition that labour embodied determines exchange value, we certainly need to refer to exchange in the proper sense—that is, to exchange between capital and labour-power. Then indeed one can see that the transition to a capitalistic economy does not allow any modification of the general law of exchange. On the other hand, when one simply confines oneself to this remark, as did Ricardo, one completely loses sight of the fact that the commodity labour-power sets free living labour greater than the labour embodied in labour power, and hence one loses the possibility of determining the origin of profit and rent. Smith, on the contrary, simply gave an incorrect representation of the exchange between capital and labour and therefore did not succeed in seeing the permanence of the general law of exchange in capitalism as well as mercantilism. Nevertheless, with his labour commanded concept, he referred to a *new* quantity of labour, which is essential to an understanding of the surplus and hence of the source of profit and rent.

6

We have seen how Ricardo overcame Smith's objection to the use of labour embodied in the theory of exchange value in a capitalistic situation. Now, however, Ricardo was able to draw the first importance consequence from the use of the labour embodied concept in this field, which consisted of the possibility of determining the rate of profit in physical terms without having recourse to the unrealistic hypothesis of the existence of a productive activity in which the product and capital are composed of a single commodity. In other words if the theory in question were true, if, that is, the relative values of exchange in a capitalistic economy were effectively equal to the ratios between the quantities of labour embodied in the goods, then the rate of profit could be determined in an analogous manner to that in the 'corn' model, with the only difference that quantities of corn would now be replaced by quantities of labour.[13] Naturally, one is not dealing with a difference of small importance: if the 'corn' model were acceptable, the determination of the rate of profit would follow immediately. If one abandoned the basic 'corn' model hypothesis, the determination of the rate of profit in physical terms would certainly remain possible, but only through the mediation of a theory of value, on the validity of which thus depends the validity of determining the rate of profit in this particular way.

Thus, to go on from here, the central problem of Ricardo's research consists in ascertaining whether, once having disposed of Smith objection, the labour embodied theory is safe from other possible objections. And here Ricardo came across very serious difficulties since the exchange of goods according to the quantities of labour embodied in them immediately appeared to him imperfectly consistent with the reality of market competition.

This non-coincidence between exchange ratios and labour embodied in commodities is illustrated by Ricardo in the fourth and fifth sections of the first chapter of the *Principles*. His treatment is not very lucid, and can give rise to considerable ambiguity. One of the major ambiguities can follow from the fact that, though he makes frequent reference to fixed capital, yet, in the examples given, the means of production that make up part of such capital (for example, machines, buildings, etc.) are always devoid of the essential characteristic that in point of fact makes them become fixed capital, *viz.*: that they transmit only *a part* of their value to the value of the annual product. In fact he treats fixed capitals as though they were eternal, so that while the value of the product contains a profit element calculated at the current rate on the value of the means of production, there is no amortisation share. And in reality, when Ricardo refers to the 'durability' of fixed capital, he nearly always means not the durability of the means of production that make up the capital, but the time that passes from the moment when a given quantity of labour is invested in the production of means of production, to the moment when these means are, in their turn, invested in the production of the good concerned.

This said, the somewhat confused argument of Ricardo may be put in the following form. If the rate of profit is equal in all activities (as must certainly happen by virtue of the competitive process), then the ratio of exchange between two goods will depend not only on the quantity of labour (direct and indirect) totally embodied in them, but also on the different ways in which the labour embodied in the goods apply to periods of investment.

Consider commodity 1, which to be produced requires a total L_1 of labour. This total quantity L_1 consists of the addition of L_{11} and L_{12}: the quantity L_{11} is the quantity of labour rendered in the current period for the production of good 1; L_{12} is the quantity of labour rendered in the previous period for the production of the means of production now necessary to produce the good in question. For simplicity we suppose that other factors of production are not necessary to produce the factors currently employed. Suppose, as Ricardo always does, that labour is paid by an (annual) advance (or annual investment of circulating capital). If w is the wage, in some unit of account, the proportion of the commodity cost imputable to direct labour is equal to the wage advances effected at the beginning of the current year, that is wL_{11}. If r is the rate of profit, this advance will contribute to the value of the commodity by an amount equal to $w(l + r)L_{11}$. The other part of the cost of the good is that imputable to the advance of the means of production; such an advance has the value $w(l + r)L_{12}$. The latter's

Ricardo

contribution to the formation of the commodity's value is thus $w(l + r)^2 L_{12}$. Hence, the total value of commodity 1 is:

$$V_1 = w(l + r)L_{11} + w(l + r)^2 L_{12}$$

Similarly, a commodity 2, that requires in total L_2 of labour, consisting of the addition of L_{21} and L_{22} will have the value:

$$V_2 = w(l + r)L_{21} + w(l + r)^2 L_{22}$$

According to the law of labour value, the ratio V_1/V_2 should be equal to L_1/L_2. But from the formulae above one is led to the result that, for this to be true, the condition $L_{11}/L_{12} = L_{21}/L_{22}$ must hold. That is, it is necessary that the time structure of embodied labour be the same for both goods. The necessity of this condition evidently rests on the fact that the profit factor that must be calculated on the value of labour embodied will be greater for a longer period than for a shorter one. For a given quantity of labour embodied there is thus in general a positive relationship between the length of the production period and a commodity's value.

The Ricardian conclusion, abstracting from the ambiguity which characterizes his exposition, may be expressed in general terms as follows. Following the formation of a general rate of profit, not only is the quantity of labour embodied of importance for the determination of relative commodity values, but also the temporal structure of such embodied labour. Hence, if these structures are different, relative values do not correspond to the ratios between quantities of labour.

A peculiar feature of Ricardo's exposition (that serves to confuse yet further an already confused text) is that he very often expresses this conclusion in the following way: in the determination of relative values not only are quantities of labour of importance, but also the *value of labour* since, if the wage changes, relative values change too, without however there being any change in labour quantities. To see what this signifies we return to the preceding formulae. First of all we must realize that w and r are not independent because, as we know, an increase in the wage rate results in a fall in the profit rate. To clarify this, let us suppose that w increases and hence r falls. If, for the two goods considered, the ratio between

L_{11} and L_{12} is equal to that between L_{21} and L_{22}, the fall in r will have no effect on the ratio between V_1 and V_2. But, if the time structures are different, the fall in r will have a greater effect on the value of the good which has a relatively greater value invested in the previous period, so that this good would experience a fall in its value compared with the other good.

It is clear that one is here confronted by an indirect method of explaining the general case in which the law of labour value is modified by the (competitive) formation of the rate of profit. Such a circumstance is in fact quite independent of wage movements. That is, it does not depend on the particular values assumed by the general rate of profit, but solely on the fact that such a rate exists. This was understood precisely by Marx, who writes 'If Ricardo had gone into this more deeply, he would have found that . . . the mere existence of a *general rate of profit* necessitates *cost prices* that differ from *values*. He would have found that, even if *wages* are assumed to *remain constant*, the difference exists and therefore is *quite independent* of the rise or fall in wages, thus he would have arrived at a new definition. He would also have seen how incomparably more important and decisive the understanding of this difference is for the whole theory, than his observations on the variation in *cost-prices* of commodities brought about by a rise or fall of wages.'[14]

7

This indirect way of putting the question is however the one which, as we have said, Ricardo adopts most frequently to show the difficulties in labour value theory. And in addition the problem is often formulated by him in a most singular form, in fact as the impossibility of finding an 'invariable measure of value'.[15] The problem is as follows: if one wishes to find a unit of account for exchange value, having the sense and function such that it can measure any physical or geometrical magnitude, one would need to identify such a unit with the value of a commodity that always requires the same quantity of labour for its production. For example, just as a unit of measure of length is a given and unchangeable distance, so should a measure of exchange value be the value of that good which always embodies the same quantity of labour. That such a good does not exist is not thought by Ricardo to be an invalidating difficulty, since what interests him is not whether a value measure can in fact be found, but only the mere possibility of defining it in such a way that it would have the necessary characteristics of such a measure. The real difficulty, for Ricardo, rests in the fact that if one values goods according to magnitudes one is usually specifying a unit of measure, and if such a unit is the value of a (hypothetical) commodity that always has the same amount of labour embodied in it, one discovers in fact that the commodity concerned can never furnish the required unit of measure. This is because other goods do not have fixed exchange relationships with the standard of value (even though the quantities of labour embodied in them do not change) when there is a change in distribution. In this sense the unit of measure would not be 'perfect', and would not in fact exist. The impossibility of defining a 'perfect' unit is a particular way of expressing the impossibility of relating exchange values with proportions of labour embodied.

Among the various writings in which Ricardo sets out the difficulties encountered in the definition of an 'invariable measure of value' there is one particularly noteworthy contribution entitled *Absolute Value and Exchangeable Value* written in 1823, a little before the author's death. For a long time unknown, it was found and published by Sraffa in 1951.[16] In this work it seems that Ricardo, wishing to measure value, when discussing those difficulties he had spoken of in the *Principles*, introduces together with exchange value the entirely new concept of absolute value, which appears to be put forward as the 'cause' of exchangeable value. This absolute value concept has been made the target of one of the more persistent criticisms that modern economics has levelled against Ricardian, and hence all classical, economics. But in reality absolute value for Ricardo is nothing but exchange value with reference to an invariable unit of measure (contrary, one must say, to what Marx will put forward). This unit of measurement is defined as a particular quantity of labour, and individual exchange values are measured with respect to this unit so that they are measured absolutely in terms of labour. Thus, all exchange values are considered as absolute magnitudes, that is in terms of total quantities of labour units via the unit commodity used as a measure.

But then absolute value, at least in Ricardo's sense, is the same as labour-value, and therefore falls under the same criticisms without giving rise to any further specific difficulty.

8

Faced by these difficulties in labour value theory, Ricardo finally simply contented himself with only an approximate determination of exchange value. In other words he continues to consider the quantity of labour embodied in commodities as the decisive element in the determination of value, not in the sense that it constitutes the unique element on which value depends, but only in the sense that it is the most important element in the determination of that value.[17] Since it is evident that in a question of this type a simple approximation cannot be allowed, for to be thus content implies the renunciation of hoping to reach an explanation of the subject examined, the Ricardian inquiry must be considered unsuccessful. This must not be taken in the sense that the problem he poses is irresolvable. The formulation of a schema within which the rate of profit is determined in physical terms, and at a stage that logically precedes the determination of values, is a problem that can be solved, as more recent economic inquiry has shown.[18] We will not go deeper into such questions here. We will instead emphasize another aspect of Ricardo's thought. In the *Principles* he upholds the same thesis he had sustained in 1815, that the rate of profit in agriculture determines the general rate of profit, and that therefore the tendency for profit rate to fall in agriculture will bring about a fall in the profit rate for the system as a whole.[19] It is important to specify under what conditions (made explicit by Ricardo) such a thesis can be maintained, given that we need a theory of value because the rate of profit in agriculture cannot be calculated independently of values.

In these new conditions, the subsistence wage (that Ricardo calls the 'natural price' of labour) has a value equal to the quantity of labour embodied in a labourer's means of subsistence. This can be supposed to increase only if one supposes that the main commodity that enters into the wage is corn (assumed to represent the total agricultural product), since only for corn can one assume a tendency for there to be an increase in the amount of labour necessary to produce it. It is precisely this argument that Ricardo develops in Chapter 6 of the *Principles*.

But it is well to bear in mind the hypothesis that is necessary to reach this conclusion. In the first place, it is necessary to assume that corn has such importance to the labourer's subsistence that its price influences in a decisive way the value of the wage.[20] In the second place it is necessary to assume that the use of means of production other than corn in agriculture has negligible importance. Only if this latter is true can one ignore the positive influence on the rate of agricultural profit that a fall in the quantity of labour embodied in the means of production would have, and the positive effect on agricultural profit that would occur if there were a fall in the quantity of direct labour employed as a result of improvements in methods and instruments of cultivation.

But if these requirements hold, one is necessarily led to a singular, but certain, conclusion. In the field of value theory, in order to arrive at the same conclusion concerning the rate of profit, one needs to accept the same hypothesis Ricardo assumed in his more simple theoretic structure of 1815. Such a hypothesis is directly contrary to that which makes it necessary to adopt a general theory of value. Thus, with respect to Ricardo's purpose, the theory of labour value shows itself to be useless, because the attainment of his purpose (the demonstration of a falling rate of profit) requires the adoption of those assumptions that enabled the rate of profit to be calculated in terms of corn, without any need to have recourse to values.

We find ourselves, then, in this situation: if we admit that the assumptions that render it possible to determine the profit rate in corn terms are unrealistic—if therefore one accepts more general assumptions—a theory of value becomes necessary. But, at the same time, these more general assumptions make invalid Ricardo's arguments intended to demonstrate a falling profit rate. If one wishes to retain such arguments, it is necessary to turn to these unrealistic assumptions, the acceptance of which makes value theory superfluous.

9

The importance of the Ricardian theory of profit (one that remains: its analytic defects derive from a non-rigorous value theory) is that it allows, for the first time in the history of economic thought, the specification in an adequate way of the terms of conflict between the landowning and bourgeois classes. We have seen that, other things being equal, if agricultural produce constitutes the larger part of products consumed by wage earners, anything that increases the price of these products also increases rent. Through the increase in value of wage goods, and hence of a wage as a cost to the capitalist, the rate of profit falls. In this event the position of the wage earners is unchanged since, according to the Ricardian hypothesis, the quantity of goods bought with the wage always stays the same, that is, the real wage for the labourer remains unchanged and corresponds to the establishment of a subsistence level. But the interests of the capitalists and landowners are diametrically opposed: the first tend to favour any circumstances that would lower the price of agricultural products and therefore labour costs; the latter would instead tend to be opposed to the emergence of such circumstances. In particular a question which could, and in fact did, accentuate the conflict between the two classes concerns the importation of corn. If an actual possibility exists of acquiring corn from another country at a lower price than it can be obtained domestically, importation would keep under cultivation only those lands for which costs, including the general profit rate, are no greater than the import price. In this way rents would be less than they would have been if total supply had been domestically produced, while the rate of profit would increase by reason of the lower cost of subsistence. It is well known that Ricardo upheld this thesis in Parliament and was among those who were to contribute to the adoption of liberal policies in England, which had such great importance in the development of English capitalism.

10

But the conflict between the landowning and bourgeois classes was not the only one considered by Ricardo, for he also succeeded in correctly appreciating the conflict between the bourgeois and the proletariat. Ricardo held, as we have said, that as a long period tendency, the wage rate is destined to be at a level of subsistence, which he conceived in substantially physiological terms. It is true that for short periods the wage rate can, in his opinion, diverge from such a level and in particular rise above it, with the result that wages would then be composed of two parts, one of which would correspond, from the point of view of the system, to a cost, while the other would represent a participation in the net product by the wage earner. But as a rule there will be no such participation with the result that, having to consider the total of goods that constitute the wage as substantially fixed, the rate of profit comes to depend on the greater or less 'difficulty of production' of wage goods. In this structure there is no place for the emergence of a conflict between masters and workers since, though the rate of profit depends on the value of the wage, the *real* position of the worker is completely independent of such value. Instead the conflict, according to Ricardo, arises in another way, and concerns employment. The problem is dealt with by Ricardo in the chapter of the *Principles* which is devoted to the distinction between gross revenue and net revenue, and also in the chapter on the machine question. He means by gross revenue 'the whole produce of the land and labour' of any country, a produce that, according to his schema, is divided into the three respective shares of wages, profit, and rent. By net produce he means gross produce less wages, and hence the sum of profits and rent. Now, a very characteristic aspect of the Ricardian position is the thesis that what is important to a country's economy is not gross product, upon which depends the system's capacity to employ labour, but net product, on which depends the nation's capability 'of supporting fleets and armies, and all species of unproductive labour'.

There are two observations that seem relevant with regard to Ricardo's formulation. In the first place, there is undoubtedly still here a residuum of the old economic models that referred to a pre-capitalistic reality and hence regarded the ends of the economic process as those of consumption. Not until Marx do pre-capitalistic elements entirely disappear. But, in the second place, the fact that gross product is considered irrelevant once the magnitude of net product is given—that it is of no importance whether a given net product resulted from a small or large gross product—is a precise index of the understanding Ricardo had of the true nature of capitalism: that it is an economy with the special characteristic that it tends to regard profit as an end in itself.

According to Ricardo, the main way in which a different size of gross or net product can be important to the working of the economic system is through the introduction of machines in the productive process. Before the third edition of the *Principles*, published in 1821, Ricardo had maintained that the introduction of machinery, though it might immediately reduce employment, did not however result in a permanent fall in the quantity of labour employed. This is because the labourers replaced by the machines will later re-enter the productive process, partly to provide for the extra needs of labour employed in machine production, and partly to sustain the increase in production that is in its turn due to the fact that the introduction of machinery, by increasing labour productivity and hence lowering the product prices, encourages an expansion of demand. In the third edition Ricardo adds a chapter on machinery, directed towards retracting his original opinion, arguing instead that the reabsorption of those initially unemployed is not a necessary consequence of the introduction of machinery, and that such introduction could bring about a permanent fall in the level of employment.

Ricardo's reasoning, based on the different relevances of net and gross product (taking the same numerical example as that in his text) can be put in the following terms:

(1) Suppose that in a certain initial year capitalists invest a total capital of £20,000 in the following way: £7,000 in fixed capital, and £13,000 in circulating capital (identified with annual wage advances). Such an investment is possible because one supposes that at the end of the previous year, and therefore at the beginning of the year considered, the economy has at its disposal (it is unnecessary here to ask how) £7,000 worth of machines, and wage goods, or necessities, to the value of £13,000. The investment in wages equal to £13,000, given the wage rate, allows the employment of a certain number of labourers. One then supposes that those labourers are only used in the production of wage goods, and we assume that the fixed capital does not depreciate and needs no labour to maintain it. If the rate of profit is 10 per cent, a capital of

£20,000 will earn £2,000, and Ricardo assumed, for simplicity, that this was entirely consumed by the capitalists. Since by hypothesis fixed capital does not contribute to the value of production, the value of production is £13,000 + £2,000 = £15,000. This value of £15,000 is what Ricardo calls 'gross product'; £2,000 of it is what he calls 'net product'. At the end of the year, therefore, the economy has (a) fixed capital of £7,000; (b) wage goods of £2,000, corresponding to profits; (c) wage goods of £13,000, available for new circulating capital.

(2) The capitalists undertake the same financial operation in the second year, that is (a) they maintain the investment of £7,000 in fixed capital, (b) they advance wages of £13,000 (they can do so because the economy possesses necessaries of equal value made available by the previous year's production). With the constant profit of £2,000, there is a new production of £15,000 (again coinciding with gross product and always including a net product of £2,000); but, in contrast to the first year, we now suppose that one half of the labourers maintained by the £13,000 of wages are used in the production of necessaries and the other half are used in machine production.

At the end of the year the system now has: (a) a fixed capital of £7,000 (inherited from past years) plus £7,500 (produced during the second year) = £14,500; (b) a quantity of necessaries corresponding to profits of £2,000; (c) an amount of necessaries available for new circulation capital of £5,500.

(3) In the third year, the capitalists dispose of the same capital of £20,000 (£14,500 fixed capital and £5,500 of necessaries, or circulating capital) but it is differently made up compared with the previous years, and can only maintain a smaller quantity of labour than in the first year. Whatever is done there will be a total production (gross product) equal to £7,500 (£2,000 profits plus £5,500 wages). Hence, the net product, which is what interests the capitalists, has remained the same, but the gross product which is what regulates employment, and hence interests the worker, has fallen.

This argument by Ricardo thus makes clear the possibility of a basic conflict between the bourgoisie and the proletariat. But it is to be observed that this conflict is not thoroughly examined by Ricardo in contrast to his treatment of the opposition between the bourgeoisie and landowners. This follows from the fact that according to Ricardo one is dealing only with a possibility, rather than inevitability, of conflict. However, the possibility that conflict will result is even less certain than may seem from the basic outline of Ricardo's argument. This will become clear when two considerations are taken into account, which were emphasized by Ricardo himself.

In the first place it can be shown that the introduction of machinery, by reducing the total quantity of labour contained in a single commodity, results in a given value corresponding to greater wealth—that is, a greater abundance of goods. This implies, returning to the example above, that in real terms a circulating capital of £5,500, available after the introduction of machinery, is not necessarily less than a circulating capital of £13,000 available before such introduction, since the means of subsistence that can be bought in the new situation with £5,500 is not necessarily less than the quantity that could previously have been bought by £13,000.

In the second place, the profit of £2,000 has also increased its purchasing power as a result of the new situation brought about by the introduction of the machinery. This implies that, if the consumption of the capitalists in real terms remains as it was previously, or increases less than proportionately to the increase in purchasing power of profits, some profit will remain available for further investment, in this way giving rise to an additional demand for labour.[21]

In reality, the reasons for a class conflict between the bourgeoisie and poletariat are much more complex and profound than Ricardo succeeded in showing and one really needs to come to Marx before they begin to be opened up and stated properly.

II

Inadequacies in Ricardo's treatment of the negative aspects of the capitalist economy, particularly as regards employment, are confirmed by the obstinacy with which he denied the possibility that the economy could experience a general overproduction crisis, or rather the possibility that there could be any cause of a fall in the profit rate apart from an increase in wages.[22] This is especially brought out in his controversy with Malthus.

The criticism that Malthus directs against the Ricardian thesis —that a general overproduction crisis is impossible—has a very close relationship with his criticism of Ricardo's labour value theory. According to Malthus, the affirmation that the value of goods depends solely on labour embodied cannot be sustained, since the difficulties that Ricardo himself had encountered in this field cannot be considered overcome. He considered that one is obliged, in this field, to take up Smith's idea of 'labour commanded', the notion, that is, that the best measure one can give for the value of a good is made up of the quantity of labour for which that good can exchange.[23] But, in capitalistic conditions, the normal value of a good includes not only the wages of the workers but also profits on account of capital advances. It therefore follows that the quantity of labour that a good can acquire at the current wage is the better measure of the 'natural and necessary conditions' of its supply, because labour commanded is greater than labour embodied. The conditions must be such that the good in question is suited to capitalistic production.

In Malthus's opinion, however, the quantity of labour commanded by a good is the expression of the intensity of demand for that good, since no other way exists to express the intensity in which goods produced through labour are demanded if not by the quantity of labour that men would be willing to supply in order to obtain a unit of the good concerned. Therefore, in order for a good to be sold at its real value, so that it can command in exchange a quantity of labour greater than labour embodied in order to cover profits at the going rate, it is necessary that the intensity of demand induces the consumers to supply, in exchange for the good in question, all the above mentioned quantity of labour commanded.

But the essential feature of Malthus's reasoning is that this last condition, though necessary, is not sufficient, in the sense that it is not enough for demand to be of a given intensity because labour commanded is duly greater than labour embodied. The consumers must also have the effective means of carrying out such labour. This second condition can be expressed by saying that a demand of necessary intensity must exist for the good as an effective demand, or paying demand, such that the number of wage units exchanged for the good concerned is really greater than the number of wage units that have been paid during the production of the good.

According to Malthus, it is just this second condition that is not necessarily fulfilled in capitalistic conditions. In illustrating this point, Malthus' argument is not altogether clear. Contradictions and obscurity make it difficult to reconstruct his thought logically. Here we will seek to schematize his discourse in order to render it coherent. First of all it is useful to observe that, on this question at least, both Malthus and Ricardo accepted the Smithian background. The idea that the conversion of income to capital is nothing other than the utilization of that income for the maintenance of productive labourers [24] was accepted; and by 'productive labourers', again following Smith, is meant those who in addition to reproducing the value of their subsistence, also produce a surplus for the owner of capital.

Having said this, let us now suppose that all the productive labourers of a country give rise to a total product valued at 100 in terms of wage units. Since profits are included in this value (for the time being we ignore rent), the wages paid to the productive labourers that have given rise to this product are, say, 60. Can the product considered be sold at its value of 100 and hence be successively exchanged for a quantity of labour corresponding to 100 wage units? The difficulty that Malthus saw was in the fact that the productive labourers with wages at their disposal could only buy a 60-unit value, while capitalists on the other hand, in so far as they are by definition inclined to save rather than to spend, cannot supply the residual demand. It would then be the case that though the intensity of demand would be such as to assure the performance of a quantity of labour corresponding to 100 wage units, effective demand on the other hand only assures the sale of that part of total product that has a value of 60 wage units. The situation would be one of general over-production and therefore of crisis.

This demand deficiency cannot be remedied, according to Malthus, by converting profit into additional capital—as classical theory would have it—in the form of demand for productive labourers. Such a demand increase would meet with additional production supplied by such productive labourers, so that the disequilibrium between supply and demand will be reproduced in exactly the same terms.

For Malthus the only escape from this difficulty lies in the fact that there are enough unproductive consumers to meet the demand necessary in the market place. Malthus' solution is certainly strange. As Ricardo pointed out, the demand provided by unproductive consumers must also be a paying or effective demand, in so far as the simple desire to consume by such a group of people would not make any contribution to the demand necessary to sell all the product at its real value. But from where are the unproductive consumers able to draw the means of payment necessary to transform their potential demand into effective demand? There are two possibilities. In the first place the unproductive consumers could be *pure consumers*, that is, people who consume without producing, such as landowners, the sovereign, the Church, and perhaps certain categories of public employees. These people can draw their purchasing power from the surplus (which would otherwise have been received as profits) either directly or through the mediation of the State. But this being the case, the consumption of *pure consumers* lowers profits in exactly the same way as an increase of productive labourers' wages. In this sense how can one say the *pure consumers* are essential to the creation of a sufficient effective demand? In fact, both the creation of an income for *pure consumers* and an increase in the wage above the subsistence level are phenomena that on the one hand lower profits which must ultimately pay for them, but on the other hand they guarantee that the residual profit is (more) effectively realized through the sale of the goods in the market.

Secondly, unproductive consumers can be *non-productive labourers* in the classical sense—for example, independent artisans or servants, who receive payment for goods sold either to capitalists or to pure consumers. If the goods they produce are acquired by pure consumers, then we may fall back on the observations already made above. If they are acquired by the capitalists, then the effect of unproductive labourers in creating effective demand can be admitted only in so far as one supposes, contrary to what Malthus thought, that capitalists themselves are not only savers but also consumers.

In substance, Malthus' error does not lie in his affirmation of the necessity of unproductive consumption for capitalistic equilibrium. His mistake was rather in thinking that such consumption must necessarily come from certain determinate social categories, that is, the old landowning classes and those persons properly pertaining to a purely mercantile system but continuing to survive within the ambit of capitalism. In reality, as the history of the capitalistic system has shown, the more important source of unproductive consumption is the wage itself. All the same, in defence of the Malthusian position one can say that, as between an increase in wages and the awarding of incomes to pure consumers, the capitalist system would tend, according to the logic of its mechanism, to prefer the second solution as that which is socially less dangerous to the system. In fact, while the pure consumers are socially akin to the bourgeoisie and will in general be their allies in the political field, the freeing of wages from a bare level of subsistence places the working class, which is directly antagonistic to the bourgeoisie, in an objective position of power which they would not otherwise have had.

The extremely rigid form in which Malthus puts forward his thesis was such, however, that he overstepped many of his intentions. As he clearly states on more than one occasion, his aim was to show that, contrary to the opinions of Smith and Ricardo, not every act of saving is advantageous to society.[25] For it is possible that when savings exceed certain limits, the output deriving from the additional capital that would hence be formed finds no market outlet, thus rendering the capital and savings that led to its creation useless. But Malthus' argument, if it were valid, would demonstrate much more than this, for one can conclude from it that overproduction crises do not simply result from excessive saving, but from *any* saving whatsoever.

Bearing this in mind, Ricardo's reply to Malthus acquires a new significance. Ricardo attempts to show that the conversion of revenue into capital, that is the re-employment of revenue for the maintenance of additional productive labourers, is always possible in itself and cannot ever give rise to an overproduction crises. Ricardo's reasoning can be expressed as follows.[26] Suppose that at the beginning of a certain period wage advances of 60 are made for a given number of productive labourers, who with this value of 60 buy a given quantity of wage goods. These wage goods were produced in the previous period, and are hence available in the period considered. During the period the labourers put to work by the wage advance of 60, produce a value of 100 that at the end of the period (which coincides with the start of the next) is used for further wage advances. 60 of these are used to advance wages to the labourers previously employed, and 40 (consisting of profit) are advanced to additional productive labourers. In this way the process can continue indefinitely without giving rise to a demand deficiency. The criticism against Malthus implied by this schema is that, contrary to what Malthus thought, it correctly acknowledges that the additional production of the extra productive labourers arrives at the market in a logical time sequence such that the labourers will be employed (the actual time sequence in the example was made chronological for simplicity only).

12

The result of the discussion between Ricardo and Malthus left the problem of overproduction crises almost untouched. In fact, Malthus put forward an untenable thesis, because if the mechanism described by him truly corresponds to an effective capitalistic reality, the process of accumulation would be quite unintelligible; and yet, Malthus' problem is a real one since overproduction crises are an intrinsic characteristic of the capitalistic economy, and unproductive consumption is the only way in which the market can overcome them. Hence it must be recognized that Malthus had the right view in his belief that only an abrogation of the strictly capitalistic mechanisms could overcome the periodic occurrence of crises of this nature. On the other hand, Ricardo's criticism of Malthus was never formulated in adequate terms, since one deduces from Ricardo's argument that any amount of accumulation would be possible in the capitalistic system, which is in direct contrast with reality.

By definition, the Malthusian thesis, according to which the quantity of saving cannot exceed certain limits without giving rise to a deficiency in demand, is correct, but Malthus was unable to prove it and Ricardo was unable to appreciate the true facts of the matter.

In effect, a similar *impasse* required, for its solution, the over-throw of the hypothesis that revenue transformed into capital will be resolved into wages of productive labourers during the same period. This view was held by both Ricardo and Malthus, following the Smithian tradition. The error contained in this idea (an error that Marx first satisfactorily resolved) hindered the clarification of the nature of investment in additional means of production, and hence distorted the entire study of the growth process. There was therefore a failure to appreciate why, with private capital owner-ship and hence a decentralized investment decision structure, it is impossible to control investments in such a way as to cover too great a divergence between social product and consumption.

When Ricardo answered Malthus by means of the simple model related above (which showed that from period to period savings can be converted into capital without limitation), he confused the formulation of certain equilibrium conditions with the specification of those real circumstances that can ensure the realization of such conditions. But in point of fact such real circumstances cannot be described so long as the way in which capital accumulates is seen only as increases in wage advances and therefore in productive consumption.

This problem has a long history in economic thought. Not even Marx thoroughly resolved it, though one can say that in Marx one finds nearly all the elements necessary to its solution.

The problem of crises in capitalism is one of the two great problems that classical political economy left to later thought. The other is the explanation of the origin of profit, given the Ricardian labour value theory. That a problem arises here is shown by the fact that if one admits that goods are exchanged according to labour embodied, one is also concerned with establishing how it is possible that the capitalist can obtain a share of the product. We appear to be faced with two equally unacceptable alternatives: (1) either one admits that labour is paid according to its value and thus receives the entire product, in which case one cannot see how profit and rent or what Smith called the two 'deductions' from the total product of labour can arise; or else (2) one asserts that these 'deductions' occur, and then one is bound to conclude that, at least in the labour market, the law of value is suspended. In fact it is the classical concept of the 'value of labour' itself that came to be criticized, since if one conceives of labour as the origin of the substance of value, there is no sense in speaking of the value of labour. Marxist analysis is necessary to this question and, with the introduction of the concept of labour-power, he clarifies the theoretical situation. And Marx examines the two basic questions left open by classical thought, those of crises and the origin of profit, by bringing them strictly together so that they constitute two aspects of the same question.

References

1. 'The produce of the earth—all that is derived from its surface by the united application of labour, machinery, and capital—is divided among three classes of the community; namely, the proprietor of the land, the owner of the stock or capital necessary for its cultivation, and the labourers by whose industry it is cultivated.

'But in different stages of society the proportions of the whole produce of the earth which will be allotted to each of these classes under the names of rent, profit, and wages will be essentially different; depending mainly on the actual fertility of the soil, on the accumulation of capital and population, and on the skill, ingenuity, and instruments employed in agriculture.

'To determine the laws which regulate this distribution, is the principal problem in Political Economy: much as the science has been improved by the writings of Turgot, Stuart, Smith, Say, Sismondi, and others, they afford very little satisfactory information respecting the natural course of rent, profit, and wages.' (*On the Principles of Political Economy and Taxation*, p. 5, vol. I of the *Works and Correspondence of David Ricardo* edited by Piero Sraffa, Cambridge, 1951.)

2. *An Essay on the Influence of a low Price of Corn on the Profits of Stock; shewing the Inexpediency of Restrictions on Importation: with Remarks on Mr Malthus' Two Last Publications 'An Inquiry into the Nature and Progress of Rent'; and 'The Grounds of an Opinion on the Policy of restricting the Importation of Foreign Corn'* (London, 1815). Now republished in vol. 4 of Sraffa's *Works and Correspondence of David Ricardo*.

3. 'In treating on the subject of the profits of capital it is neces-

sary to consider the principles which regulate the rise and fall of rent; as rent and profits, it will be seen, have a very intimate connection with each other.' (Sraffa, op. cit., vol. 4, p. 9.)

4. 'The exchangeable value of all commodities, rises as the difficulties of their production increase. If then new difficulties occur in the production of corn, from more labour being necessary, whilst no more labour is required to produce gold, silver, cloth, linen, etc. the exchangeable value of corn will necessarily rise, as compared with those things.' (Ibid., vol. 4, p. 19.)

5. Marx puts forward this thesis as follows, when he criticizes the idea of J. Mill's that it is the rate of agricultural profit that regulates industrial profit: 'The price of corn rises; as a result agricultural *profits* do not fall (as long as there are no new supplies either from inferior land or from additional, less productive investments of capital)—for the rise in the price of corn more than compensates the farmer for the loss he incurs by the rise in wages following on the rise in the price of corn—but *profits fall* in industry, where no such compensation or over-compensation takes place. Consequently the *industrial profit rate* falls and capital which yields this lower rate of profit can therefore be employed on inferior lands. This would not be the case if the old profit rate prevailed. Only because the decline of industrial profits thus reacts on the agricultural profit yielded by the worse land, does agricultural profit generally fall, and a part of it is detached in the form of rent from the profit the better land yields.' (K. Marx, *Theories of Surplus Value*, translated by Emile Burns, Lawrence and Wishart, London, 1969, Part III, pp. 99–100.)

6. See P. Sraffa, op. cit., Introduction, pp. xiv and xxxii.

7. Ibid., pp. xxxi–xxxii.

8. Ibid., vol. 6, p. 117.

9. On the *Principles of Political Economy and Taxation*, first edition, London, 1817, second edition 1819, third edition 1821; now in *Works and Correspondence*, op. cit., vol. I.

10. This thesis is certainly the basis of the Ricardian criticism of Smith, though he expresses his criticism rather differently. See *Principles*, op. cit., pp. 13–15.

11. With the qualification, as expounded at great length by Ricardo in the third section of the first chapter of the *Principles*, that the total labour embodied in a good is the sum of the labour

directly employed in its production *and* the labour, contained in the means of production, that is *indirectly* necessary to the production of the good considered.

12. In a passage of the first edition of the *Principles* Ricardo says: 'Though Adam Smith fully recognized the principle, that the proportion between the quantities of labour necessary for acquiring different objects, is the only circumstance which can afford any rule for our exchanging them one for another, yet he limits its application to "that early and rude state of society, which precedes both the accumulation of stock and the appropriation of land"; as if, when profits and rent were to be paid, they would have some influence on the value of commodities, independent of the mere quantity of labour that was necessary to their production.' (Sraffa, op. cit., vol. I, pp. 22–3 n. 3.)

13. 'It was now labour, instead of corn that appeared on both sides of the account—in modern terms, both as input and as output: as a result, the rate of profits was no longer determined by the ratio of corn produced to the corn used up in production, but, instead, by the ratio of total labour of the country to the labour required to produce the necessaries for that labour.' (Sraffa, op. cit., Introduction, p. xxxii.)

14. Marx, *Theories of Surplus Value*, op. cit., Part II, pp. 175–6. For Marx value means labour embodied and cost price the effective exchange ratio. What for Ricardo is the difference between quantities of labour proportions and relative value, is for Marx the difference between value and cost price.

15. Sraffa, op. cit., vol. I, p. 43 *et seq.*

16. *Works and Correspondence*, op. cit., p. 361 *et seq.* See pp. 358–60 for an editorial note.

17. For example: 'In estimating, then, the causes of the variation in the value of commodities, although it would be wrong wholly to omit the consideration of the effect produced by a rise or fall of labour, it would be equally incorrect to attach much importance to it; and consequently, in the subsequent part of this work, though I shall occasionally refer to this cause of variation, I shall consider all the great variations which take place in the relative value of commodities to be produced by the greater or less quantity of labour which may be required from time to time to produce them.' *Principles*, op. cit., pp. 36–7.

18. See P. Sraffa, *Production of Commodities by Means of Commodities* (Cambridge University Press, 1963).

19. 'The natural tendency of profits then is to fall; for, in the progress of society and wealth, the additional quantity of food required is obtained by the sacrifice of more and more labour. This tendency, this gravitation as it were of profits, is happily checked at repeated intervals by the improvements in machinery, connected with the production of necessaries, as well as by discoveries in the science of agriculture which enable us to relinquish a portion of labour before required, and therefore to lower the price of the prime necessary of the labourer.' (*Principles*, op. cit., p. 120.)

20. 'With the progress of society the natural price of labour has always a tendency to rise, because one of the principal commodities by which its natural price is regulated, has a tendency to become dearer, from the greater difficulty of producing it. As, however, the improvements in agriculture, the discovery of new markets, whence provisions may be imported, may for a time counteract the tendency to a rise in the price of necessaries, and may even occasion their natural price to fall, so will the same causes produce the correspondent effects on the natural price of labour.' (*Principles*, op. cit., p. 93.)

21. 'I have observed, too, that the increase of net incomes, estimated in commodities, which is always the consequence of improved machinery, will lead to new savings and accumulations. These savings, it must be remembered are annual, and must soon create a fund, much greater than the gross revenue, originally lost by the discovery of the machine, when the demand for labour will be as great as before, and the situation of the people will be still further improved by the increased saving which the net revenue will still enable them to make.' (*Principles*, op. cit., p. 396.)

22. 'No man produces, but with a view to consume or sell, and he never sells, but with an intention to purchase some other commodity, which may be immediately useful to him or which may contribute to future production. By producing, then, he necessarily becomes either the consumer of his own goods, or the purchaser or consumer of the goods of some other person. It is not to be supposed that he should, for any length of time, be ill-informed of the commodities which he can most advantageously produce, to attain the object which he has in view, namely, the

possession of other goods; and, therefore, it is not possible that he will continually produce a commodity for which there is no demand.

'There cannot, then, be accumulated in a country any amount of capital which cannot be employed productively, until wages rise so high in consequence of the rise of necessaries, and so little consequently, remained for the profits of stock, that the motive for accumulation ceases.' (*Principles*, op. cit., p. 290.)

23. T. R. Malthus, *Principles of Political Economy*, first edition, London, 1920, pp. 118–120; now in *Works and Correspondence*, op. cit., vol. II, pp. 89–91.

24. 'It must be understood that all the productions of a country are consumed; but it makes the greatest difference imaginable whether they are consumed by those who reproduce, or by those who do not reproduce another value. When we say that revenue is saved, and added for capital, what we mean is, that the portion of revenue, so said to be added to capital, is consumed by productive instead of unproductive labourers.' (*Principles*, op. cit., p. 151 n.)

'It is stated by Adam Smith, and it must be allowed to be stated justly, that the produce which is annually saved is as regularly consumed as that which is annually spent, but that it is consumed by a different set of people.' (Malthus, *Principles of Political Economy*, op. cit., p. 31; now in *Works and Correspondence*, op. cit., vol. II, p. 15.)

25. 'Adam Smith has stated, that capitals are increased by parsimony, that every frugal man is a public benefactor, and that the increase of wealth depends upon the balance of produce above consumption. That these propositions are true to a great extent is perfectly unquestionable. No considerable and continued increase of wealth could possibly take place without that degree of frugality which occasions, annually, the conversion of some revenue into capital, and creates a balance of produce above consumption; but it is quite obvious that they are not true to an indefinite extent, and that the principle of saving, pushed to excess, would destroy the motive to production. If every person were satisfied with the simplest food, the poorest clothing, and the meanest houses, it is certain that no other sort of food, clothing, and lodging would be in existence; and as there would be no adequate motive to the proprietors of land to cultivate well, not only the wealth derived

from conveniences and luxuries would be quite at an end, but if the same divisions of land continued, the production of food would be prematurely checked, and population would come to a stand long before the soil had been well cultivated. If consumption exceed production, the capital of the country must be diminished, and its wealth must be gradually destroyed from its want of power to produce; if production be in a great excess above consumption, the motive to accumulate and produce must cease from the want of will to consume. The two extremes are obvious; and it follows that there must be some intermediate point, though the resources of political economy may not be able to ascertain it, where, taking into consideration both the power to produce and the will to consume, the encouragement to the increase of wealth is the greatest.' (Malthus, *Principles of Political Economy*, op. cit., pp. 8–9; now in *Works and Correspondence*, op. cit., pp. 7–10.) Commenting on what Malthus says here of the propositions formulated by Smith, Ricardo notes: 'Mr. Malthus says these propositions are true to a great extent, but it is quite obvious he adds that they are not true to an indefinite extent. But why? because the principle of saving pushed to excess, would destroy the motive to production.

'But the argument is not about the motive to production, in that everybody is agreed—the accumulation of capital may go on so much faster than labourers can be increased, that productions must cease increasing in the same proportion as capital, from want of hands; and when they do increase, the labourers by their comparative scarcity to capital, can command so large a portion of the produce as to afford no adequate motive to the capitalist to continue to save.

'All men will allow then that savings may be so rapid and profits so low in consequence as to diminish the motive for accumulation, and finally to destroy it altogether. But the question yet remains, does not the increase of wealth depend upon the balance of produce above consumption? Can this question be answered otherwise than in the affirmative?

'It is true, says Mr. Malthus, but of this increased produce the capitalist will get so small a proportion, that he will have no motive to assist in increasing the quantity of produce. I agree with Mr. Malthus; in the distribution of the actual produce the capitalist may get so little for profit, and the labourer so much for wages, that no motive may exist for the capitalist continuing to be parsimonious. Now a dispute about the effects of parsimony is one thing, and about the *motives* for being parsimonious another.

'I should not have noticed this passage here if I did not know that it forms the most important subject for discussion in Mr. Malthus' work, and is frequently brought forward under different points of view. Mr. Malthus will be found to maintain not only the opinion, which is just, that the profits of the capitalist will be diminished by an increase of productions under the circumstances supposed; but also the opinion which is wholly inconsistent with it that the wages of the labourer will be likewise reduced. Productions altogether are increased, a selection may be freely made what those productions shall be, and yet neither the capitalist nor the labourer shall be benefited by them, although they must be awarded to one or other of them.' (*Works and Correspondence*, op. cit., vol. II, pp. 8–9.)

26. Commenting on Malthus' following proposition 'nobody will ever employ capital merely for the sake of the demand occasioned by those who work for him', Ricardo writes 'Why not? I may employ 20 workers to furnish me food and necessaries for 25, and then these 25 to furnish me food and necessaries for 30—these 30 again to provide for a greater number. Should I not get rich although I employed capital "merely for the sake of the demand occasioned by those who work for me" . . .?' (*Works and Correspondence*, op. cit., vol. II, pp. 428–9.)

Five:

Abstract Labour, Exchange and Capital in Marx

In the first book of *Capital*[1] Marx states that the 'two fold character of the labour embodied in goods' is 'the pivot on which a clear comprehension of Political Economy turns'. The point is confirmed in the letter to Engels of 24 August 1867. 'The best part of my book is: (on this rests *all* the understanding of the *facts*) the *double character of labour* set out immediately in the *first* chapter, whether it is expressed as use value or exchange value.' The importance of the distinction between 'abstract labour' and useful labour in Marx's theory of value, and the consequent difference between Marxian and Ricardian value concepts has already been thoroughly explored and we need go into it no further. Here I intend to examine the problem posed by an apparent ambiguity which one finds in Marx's presentation of the abstract labour concept. On the one hand abstract labour is deduced through an examination of exchange as such; on the other it comes to be considered as 'labour which is opposed to capital', or as wage labour. We will look at some of the more relevant passages from Marx on this question; we will go on to demonstrate that this ambiguity is apparent only; and finally the importance of this question for certain current critical interpretations of Marxism will be stated precisely.

I

Before going on to some of the passages in which Marx arrives at the classification of abstract labour by means of an examination of exchange, it might prove useful to reconsider how differently Smith and Marx treated exchange, as an indication of the gulf between Marx and classical political economy. As is well known, Smith's theoretic *schema* goes as follows: wealth depends upon the degree of labour productivity (given the proportion between productive and non-productive labourers); the degree of labour productivity depends on the division of labour, which in turn is dependent on the size of the market, that is, on the extension of exchange; 'the propensity to exchange' is assumed to be an original element, a trait of human nature, which needs no further explanation. Thus, when society develops exchange, or rather extends it from the products of the mind to material products then the system develops productivity and wealth. The society producing goods, the mercantilist society, is in Smith's view an expression of rationality and the realization of human nature. Capital, seen as subsistence advances to workers is none other than the means by which this division of labour is realized and exchange made possible.

For Marx, however, the mechanism of exchange through the mediation of things establishes relationships between 'reciprocally indifferent' individuals. In the course of their labour men become isolated and separate from each other; relationships between them are established *after* labour has been performed, through the exchange of products. Social links are not established during the outlay of living labour, but during the dead labour stage where labour has been objectified in the product as a good. For Marx, then, mercantile exchange is so little the expression of rationality and naturalness that in it the intrinsic character of human labour—*social* labour—is entirely nullified. Society is salvaged outside of the mediation of labour, when labour in fact has become nothing more than an object. Thus in contrast to societies based on interdependent personal ties, the mercantile society is a universal dependence of individuals with exchange as a social link, which in turn has been rendered independent of them.

We find, for example in the *Grundrisse* (pp. 156 *et seq.*): 'The reciprocal and all-sided dependence of individuals who are indifferent to one another forms their social connection. This social bond is expressed in exchange value, by means of which alone each individual's own activity or his product becomes an activity and a product for him; he must produce a general product—*exchange value*, or, the latter isolated for itself and individualized, *money*. On the other side, the power which each individual exercises over the activity of others or over social wealth exists in him as the owner of *exchange values*, of *money*. The individual carries his social power, as well as his bond with society, in his pocket. Activity, regardless of its individual manifestation, and the product of activity, regardless of its particular make-up, are always *exchange value*, and exchange value is a generality in which all individuality and peculiarity are negated and extinguished. This indeed is a condition very different from that in which the individual or the individual member of a family or clan (later community) directly and naturally reproduces himself, or in which his productive capacity and his share in production are bound to a specific form of labour and of product, which determine his relation to others in just that specific way.

'The social character of activity, as well as the social form of the product, and the share of individuals in production here appear as something alien and objective, confronting the individuals, not as their relationship to one another, but as their subordination to relations which subsist independently of them and which arise out of collisions between mutually indifferent individuals. The general exchange of activities and products, which has become a vital condition for each individual—their mutual interconnection—here appears as something alien to them, autonomous, as a thing. In exchange value the social connection between persons is transformed into a social relationship between things; personal capacity into objective wealth.'

Again in *Capital* (vol. I, pp. 72–3): 'As a general rule, articles of utility become commodities, only because they are products of the labour of private individuals or groups of individuals who carry on their work independently of each other. The sum total of the labour of all these private individuals forms the aggregate labour of society. Since the producers do not come into social contact with each other until they exchange their product, the specific social character of each producer's labour does not show itself except in the act of exchange. In other words, the labour of the individual asserts itself as a part of the labour of society, only by means of the relations which the act of exchange establishes directly between the products and indirectly, through them, between the producers. To the latter, therefore, the relations connecting the labour of one individual with that of the rest appear, not as direct social relations between individuals at work, but as what they really are, material relations between persons and social relations between things.'

It is worth while emphasizing the contrast with which these two passages are concerned. When the social relationship is an exchange relationship then relationships do not exist between people in so far as they work—which would make for direct social relationships between workers—but are directly between things in the form of goods. Thus, the social relationship between people is manifest as an external and antagonistic link.

The situation in which labour is immediately social and society is based not on the level of objectified labour but on the level of direct, living labour, is discussed by Marx with reference either to a pre-capitalistic or a future society. For example, we find in the *Grundrisse* (pp. 171 *et seq.*): 'The labour of the individual looked at in the act of production itself, is the money with which he directly buys the product, the object of his particular activity; but it is a *particular* money, which buys only this *specific* product. In order to be *general money* directly, it would have to be not a *particular*, but *general* labour from the outset; i.e. it would have to be *posited* from the outset as a link in *general production*. But on this pre-supposition it would not be exchange which gave labour its general character; but rather its pre-supposed communal character would determine the distribution of product. The communal character of production would make the product into a communal, general product from the outset. The exchange which originally takes place in production —which would not be an exchange of exchange values but of activities, determined by communal needs and communal purposes —would from the outset include the participation of the individual in the communal world of products. On the basis of exchange values, labour is *posited* as general only through *exchange*. But on this foundation' (that is on a different basis to exchange value) 'it would be *posited* as such before exchange; i.e. the exchange of products would in no way be the *medium* by which the participation of the individual in general production is mediated. Mediation must, of course take place. In the first case, which proceeds from the independent production of individuals . . . mediation takes place through the exchange of commodities, through exchange value and through money; all these are expressions of one and the same relation. In the second case, the *pre-supposition is itself mediated*; i.e. a communal production, communality, is pre-supposed as the basis of production. The labour of the individual is posited from the outset as social labour. Thus, whatever the particular material form of the product he creates or tries to create, what he has bought with his labour is not a specific and particular product, but rather a specific share of communal production. He therefore has no particular product to exchange. His product is *not an exchange value*. The product does not first have to be transposed into a particular form in order to attain a general character for the individual. Instead of a division of labour, such as is necessarily created with the exchange of exchange value, there would take place an organization of labour whose consequence would be the participation of the individual in communal consumption. In the first case the social character of production is *posited* only *post festum* with the elevation of products to exchange values and the exchange of these exchange values. In the second case, the *social character of production* is pre-supposed, and participation in the world of products, in consumption, is not mediated by the exchange of mutually independent labours or products of labour. It is mediated, rather, by the social conditions of production within which the individual is active.'

Having thus defined the historically determined nature of exchange, Marx goes on to deduce from it the concept of abstract labour, following a well-known procedure. When the labour of the individual is not immediately social, when, that is, it is private and independent, then the task of constituting society rests entirely on labour as an object or product. It is therefore necessary that, as well as its material characteristic as an object of use, the object must have value, that is have general purchasing power in the form of money. Thus, labour though not immediately social, becomes social in so far as it is productive of money, that is, it is made social through the product assuming a value form. Since, however, in the light of this assumption all products are equal because they are general wealth through money, all types of labour, in so far as they produce money, are also made equal and parts of a general and communal labour. Hence individual labour, that is, concrete useful and determinate labour, becomes social in as much as it is turned into its opposite, *abstract* labour. When the social relationship between men is a relationship mediated by things, and is a material link made independent of individuals such that they are subordinate to an external relationship, then individuals are social only in so far as they are generic. Separated from their own determinate labour and individuality they are social only in so far as they can be by means of abstract labour.

This point is clearly made in *Theories of Surplus-Value* (Part III, pp. 135–6): 'But the labour which constitutes the substance of value is not only uniform, simple, average labour; it is the labour of a private individual represented in a definite product. However, the product as value must be the embodiment of *social* labour and as such be directly convertible from one use-value into all others. . . . Thus the *labour of individuals* has to be directly represented as its opposite, *social* labour; this transformed labour is as its immediate opposite *abstract, general labour* which is therefore represented in a general equivalent.'

2

As an example of passages which connect abstract labour specifically to capital, rather than to the general exchange mechanism, we find in the *Grundrisse* (pp. 296–7): 'The last point to which attention is still to be drawn in the relation of capital to labour is this, that as *the* use value which confronts money posited as capital, labour is not this or another labour, but *labour pure and simple*, abstract labour; absolutely indifferent to its particular *specificity* [Bestimmtheit] but capable of all specificities. Of course, the particularity of labour must correspond to the particular substance of which a given capital consists; but since capital *as such* is indifferent to every particularity of its substance, and exists not only as the totality of the same but also as the abstraction from all its particularities, the labour which confronts it likewise subjectively has the same totality and abstraction in itself. For example, in guild and craft labour, where capital itself still has a limited form, and is still entirely immersed in a particular substance, hence is not yet *capital as such*, labour, too, appears as still immersed in its particular specificity: not in the totality and abstraction of labour *as such*, in which it confronts capital. That is to say that labour is of course in each single case a specific labour, but capital can come into relation with every *specific* labour; it confronts the *totality* of all labours δυνάμει [potentially], and the particular one it confronts at a given time is an accidental matter. On the other side, the worker himself is absolutely indifferent to the specificity of his labour; it has no matter for him as such, but only in as much as it is in fact *labour* and, as such, a use of value for capital. It is therefore his economic character that he is the carrier of labour as such—i.e. of labour as *use value* for capital; he is a worker, in opposition to the capitalist.'

The thesis is that the abstract character of labour is matched by the abstract character of capital; labour is abstract in so far as it is wage labour.

To appreciate the full extent of this thesis, it is useful to recall the difference, according to Marx, between money as money and money as capital. In simple exchange, money appears and disappears from circulation; for though it is true that the exchanger essentially produces money, as soon as he does so its only use to him is as a means of acquiring the products of others, and the end purpose of the money produced by him is the acquisition of determinate use values. Circulation is thus in the nature of an alternation of money and goods. Capital, however, is circulating money in a permanent or conserved form, since in this case money can serve as a means of acquiring new money. Only when this permanence of money occurs, and 'the use value of a product appears merely as a support of exchange value' does wealth fully assume the character of abstract wealth, and the labour which produces it the character of abstract labour.

In order to develop the implications of the thesis and to better understand its nature, one may refer to the following text in the *Grundrisse* (p. 515), in which the expression *mere labour* (die bloße Arbeit) is equivalent to abstract labour: 'The notion that production and hence society depended in all states of production on the *exchange of mere labour for labour* is a delusion. In the various forms in which labour relates to the conditions of production as its own property, the reproduction of the worker is by no means posited through *mere labour*, for his property relation is not the result but the presupposition of his labour. In landed property this is clear; it must also become clear in the guild system that the particular kind of property which labour creates does not rest on labour alone or on the exchange of labour, but on an objective connection between the worker and a community and conditions which are there before him, which he takes as his basis. These too are products of labour, of the labour of world history; of the labour of the community—of its historic development, which does not proceed from the labour of individuals nor from the exchange of their labours. Therefore mere labour is also not the presupposition of realisation [Verwertung]. A situation in which labour is merely exchanged for labour —whether in the direct living form, or in the form of the product— presupposes the separation of labour from its original intertwinement with its objective conditions, which is why it appears as mere labour on one side, while on the other side its product as objectified labour has an entirely independent existence as value opposite it. *The exchange of labour for labour . . . rests on the foundation of the worker's propertylessness.'*

The point being made is as follows: for society to be based on the exchange of the products of labour as such, and hence for social labour to be abstract labour, it is necessary for labour to be separated from the objective conditions of production so that it is no longer, as it was originally, an integral part of them. Labour, in fact, is opposed to capital. In other words an historical process has taken place such that 'the labourer already finds that the objective conditions are separate from him, as capital, and the capitalist finds propertyless labour, as estranged labour'. Since it can be said that labour's objective conditions are essential to the full realization of labour itself, when the labourer is separated from them then his labour is separated from him. And it is in and because of this separation that labour is abstract, that is, separate from individuals' subjectivity, and becomes a substance in itself of which individuals, workers, are not the personification. Which leads one to the definition given in *A Contribution to the Critique of Political Economy* (pp. 24–5): 'Labour, thus measured by time, does not appear in reality as the labour of different individuals, but, on the contrary, the various working individuals rather appear as mere organs of labour.' And again, as already stated in the *Poverty of Philosophy*: 'Therefore, we should not say that one man's hour is worth another man's hour, but rather that one man during an hour is worth just as much as another man during an hour. Time is everything, man is nothing; he is, at the most, time's carcase. Quality no longer matters. Quantity alone decides everything; hour for hour, day for day; but this equalizing of labour is not by any means the work of M. Proudhon's eternal justice; it is purely and simply a fact of modern industry.' (p. 59.)

3

In order to show that the ambiguity in Marx's definition of abstract labour is only apparent, one must bear in mind the Marxian thesis that exchange only becomes general and hence capable of forming a society, with the presence of capital. Production is mercantile in a general rather than sporadic or marginal sense, only when production is capitalistic. According to Marx if a good is on the one hand capital's premise, on the other hand it is capital's specific product; while the birth of capital presupposes the formation within an old society of determinate elements of mercantile production, it is also true that the generalization of the production of goods—the assumption of commodity form on the part of the generality of products—implies that capital has generally taken over the production process.

Let us look at this point in the unpublished *Chapter VI*, 'Goods as an elementary form of bourgeois wealth, was our starting point; the presupposition for the formation of capital. On the other hand goods now appear as the *product of capital*. This circular development of our analysis corresponds to the *historic development of capital,* one of the conditions of which is the *exchange of goods, commerce,* which in turn rests on the basis of different stages of production all having in common the fact that in them capitalist productio does not or does exist in a sporadic form. Again, the fully developed exchange of goods and the *form of the good* as a social universally necessary form of the product, is uniquely the *result of the mode of capitalistic production.* . . . Only when the working population has itself ceased to form part of the objective conditions of labour, or to appear on the market as a producer of goods, so that instead of selling the product of its labour it sells labour itself, or rather, its labour capacity, then and only then will production in all its amplitude depth and extent become the *production of goods*; only then would every product become a good and the material conditions of every sphere of production enter the market as goods. Goods in fact do not become the *general elementary form of wealth* except on the base of capitalistic production. . . . And hence it is only with the appearance of capitalistic production that use value is universally mediated by exchange value.'

Again, in *Capital* (vol. I, p. 587): 'This result' ['when social, wealth becomes to an ever-increasing degree the property of those who are in a position to appropriate continually and ever afresh the unpaid labour of others'] 'becomes inevitable from the moment there is a free sale, by the labourer himself, of labour-power as a commodity. But it is only from then onwards that commodity production is generalized and becomes the typical form of production; it is only from then onwards that, from the first, every product is produced for sale and all wealth produced goes through the sphere of circulation. Only when and where wage-labour is its basis does commodity production impose itself upon society as a whole; but only then and there does it unfold all its hidden potentiality.'

The thesis is therefore that labour does not systematically produce money except in so far as it is a commodity—labour force—and acquired by money and so governed by it. The so-called 'simple mercantile society' characterized by general exchange between independent producers, owners of means of production, is, according to Marx, impossible. If labour in fact were wholly owned by the labourer, through ownership of the objective conditions of labour itself, it would possess its essential characteristic, that of being social labour, and would therefore not *become* social through its product, that is through exchange.

To conclude this point, we may refer to the following well known extract from the *Grundrisse* (pp. 247 *et seq.*), which while it reaffirms the alienating character of exchange, at the same time stresses the impossibility for exchange to develop without capital: 'It is forgotten, on one side, that the *pre-supposition* of exchange value, as the objective basis of the whole of the system of production, already in itself implies compulsion over the individual, since his immediate product is not a product for him, but only *becomes* such in the social process, and since it *must* take on this general but nevertheless external form; and that the individual has an existence only as a producer of exchange value, hence that the whole negation of his natural existence is already implied; that he is therefore entirely determined by society; that this further presupposes a division of labour, etc., in which the individual is already posited in relations other than that of mere *exchanger*, etc. That therefore this presupposition by no means arises either out of the individual's will or out of the immediate nature of the individual, but that it is, rather, historical, and posits the individual as already *determined* by society. It is forgotten, on the other side that these higher forms in which exchange, or the relations of production which realize themselves in it, are now posited, do not by any means stand still in this simple form where the highest distinction which occurs is a formal and hence irrelevant one. What is overlooked, finally, is that already the simple forms of exchange value and of money latently contain the opposition between labour and capital etc. . . . . It is just as pious as it is stupid to wish that exchange value would not develop into capital, nor labour which produces exchange value into wage labour.'

This means that according to Marx the derivation of abstract labour from the exchange mechanism *rather than* from capital is a false exercise. In reality, exchange without capital is inconceivable. One can equally well say that abstract labour is that which produces exchange value only under unique social, that is capitalistic, conditions, as that abstract labour is wage labour in opposition to capital; and that because of such opposition abstract labour's only product is exchange value.

4

A problem still remains however. When abstract labour is defined with respect to exchange one says that in so far as it is social labour it is the opposite of useful or private labour, or rather, that abstract labour is the means by which private labour is overturned to become social. No difficulties arise in this definition as a result of calling useful labour 'private' since one is concerned with the labour of '*private individuals*' each one of whom works for himself and is separate from others during the course of his work. But if abstract labour is identified as wage labour, there remains the question of what exactly is meant by private labour. In other words, the problem is as follows: in precisely what consists the private nature of concrete labour when such labour is the worker's and is opposed to capital? For capital acts in such a way that 'co-operation itself, contracted with the process of production carried on by isolated independent labourers, or even by small employers, appears to be a specific form of the capitalist process of production', and 'co-operation ever constitutes the fundamental form of the capitalist mode of production' (*Capital*, pp. 334–5).

The problem may be resolved as follows: the private character of labour consists in the fact that the individual labours of particular workers are brought together in a collective workers' labour by means of *particular* capitals, each of which is *distinct* and *opposed* to each other and in mutual competition. It remains true that 'labour becomes general labour only through exchange'. Any capital, though it brings together a group of particular types of labour under it, does not thereby change particular labour into general or social labour. For this change to take place the mediation of the exchange of the product which that capital has created through the gathering together of the different types of labour is necessary. This is so true that the very way in which capital technically brings together different labours in the productive process (from the firm to the great industry) would be incomprehensible if one did not bear in mind the end to which capitalistic production is geared, that of value in exchange.

This means that the multiplicity of capitals, and hence competition, is an essential feature of capitalistic reality in Marx's theory. For example, we find in the *Grundrisse* (p. 414): 'Conceptually, *competition* is nothing other than the inner *nature of capital*, its essential character appearing in and realized as the reciprocal interaction of many capitals with one another, the inner tendency as external necessity. Capital exists and can only exist as many capitals and its self-determination therefore appears as their reciprocal interaction with one another.'

And again in the *Grundrisse* (pp. 650–1): 'Free competition is the real development of capital. By its means what corresponds to the nature of capital is posited as an external necessity for the individual capital. The reciprocal compulsion which the capitals within it practise upon one another, on labour, etc., (the competition among workers is only another form of competition among capitals), is the *free*, at the same time the *real* development of wealth as capital. So much is this the case that the most profound economic thinkers, such as e.g. Ricardo, *presuppose* the absolute predominance of free competition in order to be able to study and to formulate the adequate laws of capital—which appear at the same time as the vital tendencies governing over it. But free competition is the adequate form of the productive process of capital. The further it is developed, the purer the forms in which its motion appear.'

The conclusion which one reaches may be put in the following forms: the transformation of labour into general or social labour involves the mediation of the market; this mediation takes place in so far as the labours of individuals, of the workers, are brought together in reciprocally separate groups each one of which is established under a determinate capital, such groups being in opposition to each other and having an inter-relationship, which is essentially an exchange relationship. In this sense capital cannot support planning, and even less can it be an expression of it. The term 'capital planning', which some interpreters have sometimes used to indicate a given phase of capitalist development, in which capital would no longer be dominated by the law of value, appears unacceptable as homogenous to Marxism. Likewise so called non-competitive market forms are always market structures which at the moment of aggregation and attraction between particular capitals, form anew—albeit at different levels—the separation and reciprocal opposition of these capitals.

It is worth while pointing out that the thesis according to which capital is capable of self-planning is often put forward in order to demonstrate the inherent error of those positions indentifying socialism with planning. But the demonstration of this error does not in fact require the proof that planning is suitable to capitalism. It would in fact be sufficient to show that planning, in the form in which it has historically occurred, repeats a relationship between labour and its objective conditions which is modelled on that which prevails in capitalism even though the social context is non-capitalistic. This is because by reproducing the separation between labour and labour's objective conditions, planning again deprives labour of its immediately social character, and in this way removes what Marx held to be the fundamental condition of socialism.

Translator's Note

The quotations from Marx are taken from the following editions:
The Poverty of Philosophy (Foreign Languages Publishing House,
Moscow, published in Great Britain by Lawrence and Wishart,
London); *A Contribution to the Critique of Political Economy*
(translated from the Second German Edition by N. I. Stoke);
Capital: A Critical Analysis of Capitalist Production (translated by
S. Moore and E. Aveling, published by Lawrence and Wishart,
London, 1970); *Grundrisse* (translated by M. Nicolaus, published
by Pelican Books, London, 1973); *Theories of Surplus Value* (trans-
lated by C. A. Bonner and E. Burns, published by Lawrence and
Wishart, London 1951). The *'Unpublished Chapter VI of Capital'*
has been translated from the Italian as rendered in Napoleoni's
text.

Readings

One:

Two Writings by François Quesnay

The works of François Quesnay have been republished in *François Quesnay et la Physiocratie* (Institut national d'études démographiques, Paris, 1958) vol. 2: *Textes annotés* (edited by L. Salleron), and it was from this edition that we have translated the two extracts published here. The first extract (vol. 2, pp. 749–58) appeared in January 1776 in the 'Journal de l'agriculture du commerce et des finances' as a reply to Mr. H. who had, in the November 1765 number of the same 'Journal', advanced objections against the *Tableau Economique* concerning the distinction between the productive class and the sterile class (Memoire sur les avantages de l'industrie et du commerce et sur la fécondité de la classe prétendue stérile). In fact Mr. H. was Quesnay himself who according to Dupont de Nemours 'not having found sufficiently strong adversaries, was pleased to give them a helping hand under the pseudonym of Mr. H.' The 'reply' which we publish here seems to us to be one of the two texts in which Quesnay best explains, with the greatest richness of argument, the theory that productivity is exclusive to agriculture labour.

The second extract (see pp. 126 *et. seq.*) is the *Maximes générale du gouvernement économique d'un royaume agricole* of November 1767 (op. cit., pp. 949–57). Our translation includes all thirty maxims, but does not include the long note that Quesnay attached to them. They concern an almost complete, and very precise, enunciation of the physiocratic principles of political economy, that were anticipated ten years before in the analogous *Maximes de gouvernement économique* in the article *Grains* that Quesnay wrote for the *Encyclopédie*.

One should bear in mind two points: the words 'production' and 'product' are always used by Quesnay only with reference to the processes and results of agricultural activity, while for other activities he used terms such as occupations, works, and the like; the term revenue or rent is used in the physiocratic sense, and refers only to landowners' rent, gross of taxes, and tithes levied on it.

JANUARY 1766

Reply to the Report by M.H. on the Advantages of Industry and Commerce and on the Fecundity of the so-called Sterile Class, etc. included in the Journal of Agriculture, Commerce and Finance for the Month of November 1765.
By the friend of the author of this Report, or Letter to the authors, etc.

Gentlemen,

The note you have inserted on page 156 of your Journal of 15 September has become the subject of a serious discussion and is indeed worthy of being pursued. M.H. has vigorously contested this note or rather the principles of the *Economic Table* which are set forth in it. You have opposed to his concise and plausible reasonings suggestions which appear to me at least to counterbalance them, and I should very much like you or someone else to undertake the *Essay on Prices* the plan of which you have outlined in your comments and which I regard as indispensable to end disputes about this matter. But while awaiting this work which cannot be too carefully thought out if it is to be made public, I think it useful to make a preliminary reply to M.H.: and as I am certain that in addressing his Report to you his only intention was to contribute to the establishment of the truth, by the close friendship which unites us I feel certain that I also share his attitude in replying to him.

I am going to begin, therefore, by recalling here the note which indicates the state of the question.

The productive class (you state, according to the *Economic Table*) includes all men employed in work necessary to obtain the products of the land proper to men's enjoyment. This work ends with the sale of their products at first-hand. By this sale, the products pass, as raw materials, into the hands of agents of the *sterile class*, for the manufacture of articles by this class; or as merchandise into the hands of tradesmen to be transported and resold in the places where they are consumed.

The increase in price which they entail after the first-hand sale through the commercial transactions of those who resell them, or by the efforts of the other agents of the *sterile class*, is not an increase in wealth: this price increase consists only of the payment due to the agents from the non-productive class for their work and it is paid to them by what is produced by the price of the first-hand sale. It is the revenue expenditure from the owners of property resources and from those of the *productive class* to the *sterile class* which pays this remuneration to the agents of this class; and the less heavy it is the greater the profit to the income of the State and the nation. For this remuneration lowers the price of the first-hand sale, or is derived from the same product of this sale. The total income resulting from first-hand sales by the productive class in the year is the measure of the renewed wealth for that same year. The work of industry and commerce cannot extend it beyond this measure. The agricultural countries which trade among themselves are all subject to the same law. None of them gives its wealth to another except for wealth of the same value. So the work of their business men does not increase their wealth and they pay, on both sides, the increase in price resulting from the expenses inseparable from the work and the expenses of commerce and industry. The increase in costs cannot increase the wealth of those who refund these expenses: the increase in price caused by the cost of the commercial transaction is therefore not an increase in wealth for the nations which pay these costs on both sides through their reciprocal buying and selling. In this commercial exchange between nations, each can buy only as much as it sells: so their reciprocal sales and purchases reduce them to the same degree of wealth which each had, individually, before their commercial exchange: it even appears that they are less rich because they have paid the costs of both types of transaction; but they also refund these costs mutually and this reduces them all equally, or almost equally, to the measure of wealth which they had previously, supposing that, in this reciprocal business, they have taken equal care of their interests; if this is not the case, we must believe that they are merely in turn dupes of one another, which amount to the same thing. In any case, the advantage will not be on the side of those whose business will be heavily weighted in favour of manufactured goods, although these are paid for at a higher rate; for this is only a simple refund of what has been paid by them already in costs, and this does not mean an increase in wealth like something which brings about new production which assures a net profit; such an increase, apart from the consumers who live on the expenses of which it is the fruit, maintains, in addition, other consumers.

Here we have the order of expenditure, presented in the *Economic Table*, and here too is the actual object of the great debate which is being carried on between experts who write on *economic science*.

The author of the Report included in your Journal of last November does not wish to recognize this division into *productive class* and *sterile class*, with the opposing meanings these terms suggest. According to him, 'there is, through the price which purchases give to products, a circle of productive communication between the two classes which makes them equally and reciprocally fruitful in relation to each other. The class named productive in the *Economic Table* engenders productions, but it does not confer on them the price which gives them the quality of wealth'; 'it is,' he states, 'the class denoted sterile in the same *Table* which, by the purchases it makes from the productive class, procures for them the market value on which all the calculations of the *Table* are based: it is therefore to the purchases made by the sterile class from the productive class that we must attribute the wealth of a nation; so this class is not unproductive; it is therefore inappropriate to extend the limits of the productive class to the sale of products at first-hand, since the produce from these sales is provided by the so-called sterile class. Therefore, it is not to the productive class that this produce should be ascribed. The so-called sterile class is consequently as productive as the other class, since it is the source of the produce of the market value of sales of first-hand products. The limits of the productive class therefore extend only as far as the point where work which results in production from the land ends, and not to the sale of this production at first-hand. For at this limit the productive class has produced everything it can produce;

and afterwards it is the so-called sterile class which produces, through the sale of first-hand products, the market value which the productive class draws from its products: thus, the so-called sterile class is no less productive than the productive class itself.'

This specious reasoning, carried out step by step very skilfully, appears quite conclusive and alters completely the explanation of the calculations provided by the *Economic Table*.

But if one asks the author what is it that the non-productive class seems to him to have produced: what will he reply? Is it the money with which it has paid for the products it has bought from the productive class? But we know it has received this money from the sales which it also has made (*sic*) and that it has therefore not produced it.

Moreover, we know that it gains as much as possible through these sales and that it gives away as little as possible in its purchases: so in this way it contributes as much as it can to the fall in the price of the goods it buys and it tends on the other hand as far as possible to augment the prices of the goods it sells; viewed in this way, it would be producing not as a buyer but as a seller, that is to say, producing the market value which constitutes wealth: now, in the same way, the productive class will also be itself the producer of the market value of the commodities which it sells.

But all these ideas are fanciful; prices are not controlled by the interests of either the buyer or the seller; these interests themselves are mutually opposed in selling and in buying; so the seller and the buyer regarded separately are not the arbiters of the prices for products. It would be to suggest an inconceivable paradox to state that the sterile class viewed separately is productive of the market value of the products which result from the work of the productive class. For no one is unaware of the fact that the general causes of the current prices of products are their scarcity or their abundance, or the more or less intensive competition between buyers and sellers; and, for these reasons, the actual price of the goods precedes their sale, even when it is at first-hand. Now, it is on the basis of this absolute price, to which the sterile class itself is subject prior to its purchase, that in the *Economic Table* the calculations of the market value of the goods which have resulted from the work of the productive class have been established; and indeed it is on this very price that, reduced to an annual average, the farmers on properties settle the rate of the rent which they agree to pay the landowners during the period of their lease. The basis of this calculation should not be regarded as *the structure of a new system which would overthrow completely the economic order*; because this so-called *new structure* is as old as agriculture.

The author, obliged to retrench his position, will continue to hold that the *sterile class* at least contributes to the market value of the goods it buys from the productive class; but he must be aware that it contributes to this no more than the *productive class* contributes to the market value of what it buys from the *sterile class*; and that these purchases counterbalance one another on each side so that their effect on each side is reduced to exchanges of value for equal value. A value, I say, which existed on both sides before the exchange so that, in fact, the exchange produces nothing. The *sterile class*, therefore, is not *productive* through its purchases of the value of the goods it buys from the productive class. It is the same in the case of the productive class in relation to what it buys from the sterile class; for on each side they are equally buyers and sellers and are mutually subject to the same conditions and laws of exchange.

The author may think he is mistaken and that it is as seller that the so-called sterile class is productive, since the value of what it sells existed even prior to the sale, because in these sales there is an exchange of value for equal value. But in relation to the question with which we are concerned here, we must distinguish the value of renewed production from the value of expenditure purely as costs; for expenditure is not production; and the refund of this expenditure, when it is not the result of the renewal of wealth produced by Nature, is in itself only a new expense which is no more a product than the expenditure of costs was one. So, in sales by the sterile class, this class sells only values of simple expenses as costs. But since it is clear that expenditure merely as costs is not production, it is equally clear that the sterile class, as it sells only values of simple expenses as costs, does not produce the price of these sales.

We shall doubtless be asked if an artisan who sells his work, for example a shoemaker who sells a pair of shoes, only sells a value of simple expenditure as costs? A shoemaker who sells a pair of shoes sells both the raw material from which he has made the pair of shoes and his work, the value of which is determined by that of his expenditure on goods or articles necessary for the subsistence and maintenance of his family and himself during the time employed in making the pair of shoes: here we see merely consumption and no production. But, you may say, *is there not the production of a pair of shoes?* No, for if you distinguish between the raw material of this pair of shoes and the fashioning of this article you will find only the workmanship carried out by the toil of the shoemaker, the value of which is in the simple expenditure in costs for his subsistence; and if you ask him what is the fashioning for which he wishes to charge a price, he will tell you that it is his work used in making the pair of shoes. For a workman will say variously that he charges for his workmanship, his time, his toil, his costs; all these terms are to him synonymous.

It would still remain for us to say that *this work at least produces subsistence for the workman and his family.* But there is no indication that there is any intention of misusing words in such a way as to suggest that a simple consumption is production. For production, as we understand it here, is a renewal of certain wealth, whereas simple consumption is the destruction of certain wealth; it is difficult to reconcile in the same notion two such contradictory things. In any case, it would be a very complicated notion which would need to be developed in order to dispel its confusion. The workman speaks more precisely: he says that he *earns* his subsistence and does not say that he *produces* it.

But would there not be some production relative to the raw materials which are employed in the work of the sterile class? This is something we must examine closely. We notice at first that the workman does not produce the raw material of his work, that he buys it and resells it with the article and in this way he could be regarded as a reseller, so the profit he would make in this resale would be taken from the person who buys the article, or from the person who has sold the raw material, and the latter would have suffered a diminution in the price of what he sold; so there would be no production in the transaction, there would be only the expenses paid by the buyer or by the initial seller.

But does not the raw material draw its market value from the use the workman makes of it? What would be the use of flax, for example, and what would be its market value of it were it not used by the weaver to make cloth? I admit that in this hypothetical case it would perhaps have no value and that the grower would stop growing it; but the land would not lie fallow: for land which produces flax can equally produce other products of high value and even certain products which do not need the work of the sterile class worker: such would be corn, wine, etc. It is really the use of the land which the grower sells to those who buy his products: and provided that the land is well used, he does not care whether he grows one product or another. Moreover, in the case in which a product would increase in price because of its use by the sterile class, the growers would increase its production so much that its price would soon no longer exceed that of the other products when all the expenses and profits were taken into account. So the use of a country's products in raw materials by the sterile class can scarcely increase the price of these products except for a short period.

But does not the variety of productions contribute to making the use of the land more secure and profitable? In addition, is not an increase in good products an increase in wealth? Here we merely observe that the use of the land would be more widely shared between several good products without increasing the total amount of production.

The quality of land is so varied that it is only by varying productions that the proper use of land can be assured: this is true: but independently of *raw material for luxury articles* there is a great variety of products using different qualities of land; the *raw materials for luxury goods* provided by cultivation are so limited that the land which would be deprived of them would not be any the less well used for other products. I mention *raw materials for luxury goods* provided by cultivation, for in every country where cultivation provides great wealth the materials for essential goods will never be lacking. Necessity alone is the father of industry, it encourages the worker to turn to it to earn his living and it also encourages all those who can buy to obtain goods. Politics need not attempt to join necessity in order to excite men to satisfy themselves in this matter, because the sterile class will always increase in proportion to the country's wealth. I say, *in proportion to the country's wealth*, since as this class produces nothing and works only for consumption, it can survive only through the nation's wealth, that is, through the resources which are created by the productive class.

Although necessity sufficiently spurs on men who can live only through their work to devote themselves to industry and to the commerce of re-sale without being spurred on by the government; although in general the work of the sterile class is less laborious than that of the productive class; although the sterile class attracts people to the cities where living conditions are preferable to those in the country, and the old proverb, '*beati qui habitant urbes*' does not allow us to ignore the fact that the sterile class is always the most complete and the most attractive section of a nation: these reasons in themselves cause people to think even more that it increases its industry and work greatly, and that it uses a great deal of material for the manufacture of goods, and that this use of raw materials should increase the output and the price of the products with which the productive class provides it. So, from this point of view, this class should not be regarded as essentially sterile.

We shall also observe that from this very point of view it has to be careful not to multiply its products beyond what it can sell. Now, it can sell them only in proportion to the nations' wealth being produced annually by the efforts of the productive class; and if it brings about an increase in the price of the materials it obtains from this class it will itself raise the cost of the goods it sells all the more; and this will, in this circular way, produce only an illusory increase in wealth. Moreover, these materials purchased from the productive class constitute such an unimportant part in the general order of cultivation of a great tract of land that only a small change in their price would result, and no important effect in relation to the total amount of reproduction of the nation's annual resources. To be exact, one would make an exception, in this general observation, of the use of wool, a good price for which gives a return to the productive class, very advantageous to agriculture: but that would depend less on the sterile class than on the restriction of luxury materials with which this class is occupied to the detriment of the consumption of woollen goods.

Even in this hypothetical raising of prices for the raw materials for the goods produced by the non-productive class, we cannot suggest that the sale of these goods to foreigners will bring about this supposed increase in wealth; for the increase in the price of these same goods which the sterile class itself would cause would stop their sale abroad. It could not therefore be brought about in a country where there would be no easy outlet for the sale of its products abroad and where their sale would be procured by the multiplication of the work of industry; here again the means and the cause must not be confused. But unfortunate would be the nations reduced to such straits, and fortunate those where no such problems exist because of the ease of their foreign trade which keeps their produce at a price that is too high to allow their sterile class to go into competition for the sale of its goods abroad, and where this class would be restricted, or almost restricted for this reason, to the selling of its goods at home.

There is an argument which is being repeated constantly and which is thought to be conclusive in favour of the opulent fecundity of industry; but when it is examined in depth it means something different from what it is intended to mean and proves the opposite of what it is intended to prove. *It is said that the more consumers there are in a kingdom the more they raise the price of the country's products and give them the quality of wealth. Now the more men are occupied in industry in a kingdom the more consumers there are.* Therefore, etc.

In academic circles the major premise would be curtly denied, but let us be satisfied in pointing out that instead of saying '*the more consumers there are*', we should say, '*the more consumption there is*', for there is no lack of consumers anywhere: everywhere the greatest number of consumers cannot consume as much as they wish; those who eat only black rye bread and drink only water would like to eat wheaten bread and drink wine; those who cannot eat meat would like to be able to eat it; those who have only poor clothing would like to have good clothing; those who have no firewood to keep them warm would like to be able to buy some, etc. So it is not consumers who are lacking, but consumption.

Now it is clear that the more superfluous expenses and efforts are cut back in the sterile class' manufacture of luxury goods and in its purchase of raw materials from abroad and these expenses and efforts used to stimulate new production, the more consumable products and especially food products would be available. If this were the case, there would then be a greater consumption, since there would be more products to consume.

The consumers, therefore, who simply aim at a greater ability to consume would increase in number and in consumption: the wealth, the revenues, the population, and the power of the kingdom would increase with the increase in cultivation and in consumption. But the more the consumption and the wealth would increase, the greater, in this case, would be the need for the services of agents from the sterile class, since their employment would be constantly multiplied in proportion to the means available to pay them: means which would increase perceptibly and become available to the agents of the productive class and to the owners of the net product from cultivation who are the owners of the land, the State and the tithe-owners, relative to the greater abundance of exchangeable products from which this greater consumption derives. The sterile class itself would consequently grow, following the result of the reduction in superfluous expenses made to this class: and it is as natural for the multiplying of wealth and of consumable goods to increase the number of consumers as it would be absurd to believe that the employment of men and of wealth in work which does not result in production, and which would be multiplied to the detriment of the expenses and work which do result in production, would nevertheless multiply production, wealth, and consumers. It is this point which must decide the question, since it proves that the sterile class is a burden on the productive class, far from enriching it or enriching the nation. Nothing reveals better the sterility and more than sterility of this class than observing that the more it extends through the increase in the cost of manufacture, transport, carriage, etc., the more it is a burden on the productive class. It cannot be said that the more it is cut back by the diminution of all these costs, the more the number of *consumers* would be restricted; because the more the work of the productive class would increase through the restriction of the work of the sterile class, the more this would be concerned with the *consumers*. So it is not through industry that the productive class can be made more prosperous and the kingdom made wealthy; it is through the productive class and through the wealth it creates that the number of men increases, the kingdom becomes opulent and the sterile class itself grows.

As for what the author has said in favour of commerce, to prove that it is productive, he could say as much in favour of the roads needed for the cartage of these products, and he would doubtless prove to us that it is the roads which produce the harvests. With the artful arrangement and combining of ideas one can prove anything to those who do not examine anything deeply. *Grain*, he said, *had fallen into non-value through the ill-considered prohibition against exporting it outside the realm*, etc. If we suppose an ill-considered prohibition against allowing carts to move along the roads we can easily parody the author's reasoning. So we need not feel obliged to argue with him.

Commerce is an exchange of things which exist and which have their respective values in terms of one another. In addition, there is a need for exchange, for without it there could be no commerce or barter; all these things precede the act of exchanging: exchange or commerce does not result in production: the action of exchanging therefore produces nothing: it is necessary only to satisfy the need which in itself is the cause of the exchange. We must therefore distinguish here between what is merely necessary and what is productive; if what is productive is necessary, it does not follow, as the author suggests, that everything that is necessary is productive. Confusion is the asylum of sophistry and discernment is the investigator who uncovers it.

The 'General Maxims for the Economic Government of an Agricultural Kingdom'

I

That there should be a single sovereign authority, standing above all the individuals in the society and all the unjust undertakings of private interests; for the object of dominion and allegiance is the security of all and the lawful interest of all. The view that there should be a balance of forces in government is a disastrous one, leaving scope for nothing but dissension among the great and the oppression of the small. The division of societies into different orders of citizens, some of whom exercise sovereign authority over the others, destroys the general interest of the nation and ushers in the conflict of private interests between the different classes of citizens. Such a division would play havoc with the order of government in an agricultural kingdom which ought to reconcile all interests for one main purpose—that of securing the prosperity of agriculture, which is the source of all the wealth of the state and that of all its citizens.

II

That the nation should be given instruction in the general laws of the natural order, which constitute the form of government which is self-evidently the most perfect. The study of human jurisprudence is not sufficient to make a statesman; it is necessary that those who are destined for administrative positions should be obliged to make a study of the natural order which is most advantageous to men combined together in society. It is also necessary that the practical knowledge and insight which the nation acquires through experience and reflection should be brought together in the general science of government, so that the sovereign authority, always guided by what is self-evident, should institute the best laws and cause them to be scrupulously observed, in order to provide for the security of all and to attain to the greatest degree of prosperity possible for the society.

III

That the sovereign and the nation should never lose sight of the fact that the land is the unique source of wealth, and that it is agriculture which causes wealth to increase. For the growth of wealth ensures the growth of the population; men and wealth cause agriculture to prosper, expand trade, stimulate industry, and increase and perpetuate wealth. Upon this abundant source depends the success of all branches of the administration of the kingdom.

IV

That the ownership of landed property and movable wealth should be guaranteed to those who are their lawful possessors; for SECURITY OF OWNERSHIP IS THE ESSENTIAL FOUNDATION OF

THE ECONOMIC ORDER OF SOCIETY. In the absence of surety of ownership the territory would remain uncultivated. It would have neither proprietors nor farmers to make the expenditure necessary to improve and cultivate it, if protection of funds and products were not guaranteed to those who make the advances of this expenditure. It is the security of permanent possession which stimulates labour and the employment of wealth in the improvement and cultivation of the land and in commercial and industrial enterprises. It is only the sovereign power which guarantees the property of its subjects which has a right to the first share of the fruits of the land, the unique source of wealth.

V

That taxes should not be destructive or disproportionate to the mass of the nation's revenue; that their increase should follow the increase of the revenue; and that they should be laid directly on the net product of landed property, and not on men's wages, or on produce where they would increase the costs of collection, operate to the detriment of trade, and destroy every year a portion of the nation's wealth. That they should also not be taken from the wealth of the farmers of landed property; for the ADVANCES OF A KINGDOM'S AGRICULTURE OUGHT TO BE REGARDED AS IF THEY WERE FIXED PROPERTY REQUIRING TO BE PRESERVED WITH GREAT CARE IN ORDER TO ENSURE THE PRODUCTION OF TAXES, REVENUE AND SUBSISTENCE FOR ALL CLASSES OF CITIZENS. Otherwise taxation degenerates into spoliation, and brings about a state of decline which very soon ruins the state.

VI

That the advances of the cultivators should be sufficient to enable the greatest possible product to be annually regenerated by expenditure on the cultivation of the land; for if the advances are not sufficient, the expenses of cultivation are proportionately higher and yield a smaller net product.

VII

That the whole of the sum of revenue should come back into the annual circulation, and run through it to the full extent of its course; and that it should never be formed into monetary fortunes, or at least that those which are formed should be counterbalanced by those which come back into circulation. For otherwise these monetary fortunes would check the distribution of a part of the annual revenue of the nation, and hold back the money stock of the kingdom to the detriment of the return of the advances of cultivation, the payment of the artisans' wages and the consumption which ought to be carried on by the different classes of men who follow remunerative occupations. Such an interception of the money stock would reduce the reproduction of revenue and taxes.

VIII

That the government's economic policy should be concerned only with encouraging productive expenditure and trade in raw produce, and that it should refrain from interfering with sterile expenditure.

IX

That the nation which has a large territory to cultivate, and the means of carrying on a large trade in raw produce, should not extend too far the employment of money and men in manufacturing and trading in luxury goods, to the detriment of the work and expenditure involved in agriculture; for more than anything else THE KINGDOM OUGHT TO BE WELL FURNISHED WITH WEALTHY CULTIVATORS.

X

That no part of the sum of revenue should pass into the hands of foreign countries without return in money or commodities.

XI

That the desertion of inhabitants who would take their wealth out of the kingdom should be avoided.

XII

That the children of rich farmers should settle down in the countryside, so that there are always husbandmen there; for if they are harassed into abandoning the countryside and settling in the towns, they take their fathers' wealth which used to be employed in cultivation. IT IS NOT SO MUCH MEN AS WEALTH WHICH OUGHT TO BE ATTRACTED TO THE COUNTRYSIDE; for the more wealth is employed in cultivation, the fewer men it requires, the more it prospers, and the more revenue it yields. Such, for example, in the case of corn is the large-scale cultivation carried on by rich farmers in comparison with the small-scale cultivation carried on by poor métayers who plough with the aid of oxen or cows.

XIII

That each person should be free to cultivate in his fields such produce as his interests, his means, and the nature of the land suggest to him, in order that he may extract from them the greatest possible product. Monopoly in the cultivation of landed property should never be encouraged, for it is detrimental to the general revenue of the nation. The prejudice which leads to the encouragement of an abundance of produce of primary necessity in preference to other produce, to the detriment of the market value of one or the other, is inspired by short-sighted views which do not extend as far as the effects of mutual external trade, which makes provision for everything and determines the price of the produce which each nation can cultivate with the most profit. AFTER THE WEALTH EMPLOYED IN CULTIVATION, IT IS REVENUE AND TAXES WHICH ARE THE WEALTH OF PRIMARY

NECESSITY in a state, in order to defend subjects against scarcity and against the enemy, and to maintain the glory and power of the monarch and the prosperity of the nation.

XIV

That the breeding of live-stock should be encouraged, for it is live-stock which provides the land with the manure which procures abundant crops.

XV

That the land employed in the cultivation of corn should be brought together, as far as possible, into large farms worked by rich husband-men; for in large agricultural enterprises there is less expenditure required for the upkeep and repair of buildings, and proportionately much less cost and much more net product, than in small ones. A multiplicity of small farmers is detrimental to the population. The population whose position is most assured, and which is most readily available for the different occupations and different kinds of work which divide men into different classes, is that maintained by the net product. All economies profitably made use of in work which can be done with the aid of animals, machines, rivers, etc., bring benefit to the population and the state, because a greater net product procures men a greater reward for other services or other kinds of work.

XVI

That no barriers at all should be raised to external trade in raw produce; for AS THE MARKET IS, SO IS THE REPRODUCTION.

XVII

That the marketing and transport of produce and manufactured commodities should be facilitated, through the repair of roads and the navigation of canals, rivers, and the sea; for the more that is saved on trading costs, the more the territory's revenue increases.

XVIII

That the prices of produce and commodities in the kingdom should never be made to fall; for then mutual foreign trade would become disadvantageous to the nation. AS THE MARKET VALUE IS, SO IS THE REVENUE: *Abundance plus valuelessness does not equal wealth. Scarcity plus dearness equals poverty. Abundance plus dearness equals opulence.*

XIX

That it should not be believed that cheapness of produce is profitable to the lower classes, for a low price of produce causes a fall in the wages of the lower orders of people, reduces their well-being, makes less work and remunerative occupations available for them, and destroys the nation's revenue.

XX

That the well-being of the latter classes of citizens should not be reduced; for then they would not be able to contribute sufficiently to the consumption of the produce which can be consumed only within the country, which would bring about a reduction in the reproduction and revenue of the nation.

XXI

That the proprietors and those engaged in remunerative occupations should not give themselves over to sterile savings, which would deduct from circulation and distribution a portion of their revenue or gains.

XXII

That no encouragement at all should be given to luxury in the way of ornamentation to the detriment of the expenditure involved in the operations and improvement of agriculture, and of expenditure on the consumption of subsistence goods, which sustains the market for raw produce, its proper price, and the reproduction of the nation's revenue.

XXIII

That the nation should not suffer any loss in its mutual trade with foreign countries, even if this trade were profitable to the merchants who made gains out of their fellow-citizens on the sale of the commodities which were imported. For then the increase in the fortunes of these merchants would bring about a deduction from the circulation of the revenue, which would be detrimental to distribution and reproduction.

XXIV

That people should not be taken in by a seeming advantage in mutual trade with foreign countries, through judging it simply with reference to the balance of the sums of money involved and not examining the greater or lesser profit which results from the particular commodities which are sold and purchased. For the loss often falls on the nation which receives a surplus in money, and this loss works to the detriment of the distribution and reproduction of the revenue.

XXV

That complete freedom of trade should be maintained; for THE POLICY FOR INTERNAL AND EXTERNAL TRADE WHICH IS THE MOST SECURE, THE MOST CORRECT, AND THE MOST PROFITABLE FOR THE NATION AND THE STATE, CONSISTS IN FULL FREEDOM OF COMPETITION.

XXVI

That less attention should be paid to augmenting the population than to increasing the revenue; for the greater well-being which a high revenue brings about is preferable to the greater pressure of subsistence needs which a population in excess of the revenue entails; and when the people are in a state of well-being there are more resources to meet the needs of the state and also more means to enable agriculture to prosper.

XXVII

That the government should trouble itself less with economizing than with the operations necessary for the prosperity of the kingdom; for very high expenditure may cease to be excessive by virtue of the increase of wealth. But abuses must not be confused with simple expenditure, for abuses could swallow up all the wealth of the nation and the sovereign.

XXVIII

That the administration of finance, whether in the collection of taxes or in the expenditure of the government, should not bring about the formation of monetary fortunes, which steal a portion of the revenue away from circulation, distribution, and reproduction.

XXIX

That means to meet the extraordinary needs of a state should be expected to be found in the prosperity of the nation and not in the credit of financiers; for MONETARY FORTUNES ARE A CLANDESTINE FORM OF WEALTH WHICH KNOWS NEITHER KING NOR COUNTRY.

XXX

That the state should avoid contracting loans which create rentier incomes, which burden it with devouring debts, and which bring about a trade or traffic in finance, through the medium of negotiable bills, the discount on which causes a greater and greater increase in sterile monetary fortunes. These fortunes separate finance from agriculture, and deprive the countryside of the wealth necessary for the improvement of landed property and for the operations involved in the cultivation of the land.

Two:

The 'Glasgow Lectures' of Adam Smith

We publish here an extract from the lectures given by Adam Smith in the University of Glasgow. In 1763, a student made notes of these lectures, discovered in 1895 by Edwin Cannan, who published them in the following year under the title *Lectures on Justice, Police, Revenue and Arms, delivered in the University of Glasgow by Adam Smith reported by a student in 1763.*

After a short introduction the *Lectures* consisted of five parts—Part I: 'Of Justice', Part II: 'Of Police', Part III: 'Of Revenue', Part IV: 'Of Arms', and Part V: 'Of the Laws of Nations'. The extract presented here is taken from Division II of Part II called 'Cheapness or Plenty', and comprises the full text of the first seven of the sixteen paragraphs that make up this Division.

To appreciate how the *Lectures* represent a preparatory phase of the *Wealth of Nations* one needs to compare the reading presented here with Smith's treatment of the same material in his more mature work, that is, with the first seven chapters of Book I of the *Wealth of Nations*. Such a comparison shows that many of the examples given in the *Wealth of Nations* substantially follow the exposition offered in the *Lectures*, thus maintaining the latter's reference to a pre-capitalistic economy. However, especially as regards the analysis of the component parts of the natural price of goods, concepts arise in the *Wealth of Nations* which are still absent in the *Lectures*, in particular the tripartite class division of society into landowners, capitalists, and labourers, and the corresponding division of the social product into rent, profits, and wages.

CHEAPNESS OR PLENTY

I Of the Natural Wants of Mankind

In the following part of this discourse we are to confine ourselves to the consideration of cheapness or plenty, or, which is the same thing, the most proper way of procuring wealth and abundance. Cheapness is in fact the same thing with plenty. It is only on account of the plenty of water that it is so cheap as to be got for the lifting; and on account of the scarcity of diamonds (for their real use seems not yet to be discovered) that they are so dear. To ascertain the most proper method of obtaining these conveniences it will be necessary to show first wherein opulence consists, and still previous to this we must consider what are the natural wants of mankind which are to be supplied; and if we differ from common opinions, we shall at least give the reasons for our non-conformity.

Nature produces for every animal everything that is sufficient to support it without having recourse to the improvement of the original production. Food, clothes, and lodging are all the wants of any animal whatever, and most of the animal creation are sufficiently provided for by nature in all those wants to which their condition is liable. Such is the delicacy of man alone, that no object is produced to his liking. He finds that in everything there is need of improvement. Though the practice of savages shows that his food needs no preparation, yet, being acquainted with fire, he finds that it can be rendered more wholesome and easily digested, and thereby may preserve him from many diseases which are very violent among them. But it is not only his food that requires this improvement; his puny constitution is hurt also by the intemperature of the air he breathes in, which, though not very capable of improvement, must be brought to a proper temperament for his body, and an artificial atmosphere prepared for this purpose. The human skin cannot endure the inclemencies of the weather, and even in those countries where the air is warmer than the natural warmth of the constitution, and where they have no need of clothes, it must be stained and painted to be able to endure the hardships of the sun and rain. In general, however, the necessities of man are not so great but that they can be supplied by the

unassisted labour of the individual. All the above necessities everyone can provide for himself, such as animals and fruits for his food,
and skins for his clothing.

As the delicacy of a man's body requires much greater provision
than that of any other animal, the same or rather the much greater
delicacy of his mind requires a still greater provision to which all
the different arts (are) subservient. Man is the only animal who is
possessed of such a nicety that the very colour of an object hurts
him. Among different objects a different division or arrangement
of them pleases. The taste of beauty, which consists chiefly in the
three following particulars, proper variety, easy connexion, and
simple order—is the cause of all this niceness. Nothing without
variety pleases us; a long uniform wall is a disagreeable object. Too
much variety, such as the crowded objects of a parterre, is also
disagreeable. Uniformity tires the mind; too much variety, too far
increased, occasions an over great dissipation of it. Easy connexion
also renders objects agreeable; when we see no reason for the
contiguity of the parts, when they are without any natural connexion, when they have neither a proper resemblance nor contrast,
they never fail of being disagreeable. If simplicity of order be not
observed, so as that the whole may be easily comprehended, it
hurts the delicacy of our taste. Again, imitation and painting render
objects more agreeable. To see upon a plain, trees, forests, and
other such representations, is an agreeable surprise to the mind.
Variety of objects also renders them agreeable. What we are every
day accustomed to does but very indifferently affect us. Gems and
diamonds are on this account much esteemed by us. In like manner
our pinchbeck and many of our toys were so much valued by the
Indians, that in bartering their jewels and diamonds for them they
thought they had made by much the better bargain.

2 *That all the Arts are subservient to the Natural Wants of Mankind*

Those qualities, which are the ground of preference, and which
give occasion to pleasure and pain, are the cause of many insignifi-
cant demands, which we by no means stand in need of. The whole
industry of human life is employed not in procuring the supply of
our three humble necessities, food, clothes, and lodging, but in

procuring the conveniences of it according to the nicety and delicacy of our taste. To improve and multiply the materials, which are the principal objects of our necessities, gives occasion to all the variety of the arts.

Agriculture, of which the principal object is the supply of food, introduces not only the tilling of the ground, but also the planting of trees, the producing of flax, hemp, and innumerable other things of a similar kind. By these again are introduced different manufactures, which are so very capable of improvement. The metals dug from the bowels of the earth furnish materials for tools, by which many of these arts are practised. Commerce and navigation are also subservient to the same purposes by collecting the produce of these several arts. By these again other subsidiary (arts) are occasioned. Writing, to record the multitude of transactions, and geometry, which serves many useful purposes. Law and government, too, seem to propose no other object but this; they secure the individual who has enlarged his property, that he may peaceably enjoy the fruits of it. By law and government all the different arts flourish, and that inequality of fortune to which they give occasion is sufficiently preserved. By law and government domestic peace is enjoyed and security from the foreign invader. Wisdom and virtue too derive their lustre from supplying these necessities. For as the establishment of law and government is the highest effort of human prudence and wisdom, the causes cannot have a different influence from what the effects have. Besides, it is by the wisdom and probity of those with whom we live that a propriety of conduct is pointed out to us, and the proper means of attaining it. Their valour defends us, their benevolence supplies us, the hungry is fed, the naked is clothed, by the exertion of these divine qualities. Thus, according to the above representation, all things are subservient to supplying our threefold necessities.

3 *That Opulence arises from the Division of Labour*

In an uncivilized nation, and where labour is undivided, everything is provided for that the natural wants of mankind require; yet, when the nation is cultivated and labour divided, a more liberal provision is allotted them; and it is on this account that a common day labourer in Britain has more luxury in his way of living than an Indian sovereign. The woollen coat he wears requires very considerable preparations—the wool-gatherer, the dresser, the spinster, the dyer, the weaver, the tailor, and many more, must all be employed before the labourer is clothed. The tools by which all this is effectuated employ a still greater number of artists—the loom-maker, miln-wright, rope-maker, not to mention the brick-layer, the tree-feller, the miner, the smelter, the forger, the smith, etc. Besides his dress, consider all his household furniture, his coarse linens, his shoes, his coals dug out of the earth or brought by sea, his kitchen utensils and different plates, those that are employed in providing his bread and beer, the sower, the brewer, the reaper, the baker, his glass windows and the art required in preparing (them) without which our northern climate could hardly be inhabited. When we examine the conveniences of the day labourer, we find that even in his easy simple manner he cannot be accommodated without the assistance of a great number, and yet this is nothing compared with the luxury of the nobility. A European prince, however, does not so far exceed a commoner, as the latter does the chief of a savage nation. It is easy to conceive how the rich can be so well provided for, as they can direct so many hands to serve their purposes. They are supported by the industry of the peasant. In a savage nation every one enjoys the whole fruit of his own labour, yet their indigence is greater than anywhere.

It is the division of labour which increases the opulence of a country.

In a civilized society, though there is a division of labour, there is no equal division for there are a good many who work none at all. The division of opulence is not according to the work. The opulence of the merchant is greater than that of all his clerks, though he works less; and they again have six times more than an equal number of artisans who are more employed. The artisan who works at his ease within doors has far more than the poor labourer who trudges up and down without intermission. Thus, he who as it were bears the burden of society, has the fewest advantages.

4 *How the Division of Labour multiplies the Product*

We shall next show how this division of labour occasions a multiplication of the product, or, which is the same thing, how opulence
arises from it. In order to do this let us observe the effect of the
division of labour in some manufactures. If all the parts of a pin
were made by one man, if the same person dug the ore, [s]melted
it, and split the wire, it would take him a whole year to make one
pin, and this pin must therefore be sold at the expense of his
maintenance for that time which, taking [it] at a moderate com-
putation would at least be six pounds for a pin. If the labour is so
far divided that the wire is ready-made, he will not make above
twenty per day, which, allowing ten pence for wages, makes the pin
a half-penny. The pin-maker therefore divides the labour among a
great number of different persons; the cutting, pointing, heading,
and gilding are all separate professions. Two or three are employed
in making the head, one or two in putting it on, and so on, to the
putting them in the paper, being in all eighteen. By this division
every one can with great ease make 2,000 a day. The same is the
case in the linen and woollen manufactures. Some arts, however,
there are which will not admit of this division and therefore they
cannot keep pace with other manufactures and arts. Such are
farming and grazing. This is entirely owing to the return of the
seasons, by which one man can only be for a short time employed
in any one operation. In countries where the season[s] do not make
such alterations it is otherwise. In France the corn is better and
cheaper than in England. But our toys, which have no dependence
on the climate, and in which labour can be divided, are far
superior to those of France.

When labour is thus divided, and so much done by one man in
proportion, the surplus above their maintenance is considerable,
which each man can exchange for a fourth of what he could have
done if he had finished it alone. By this means the commodity
becomes far cheaper, and the labour dearer. It is to be observed
that the price of labour by no means determines the opulence of
society; it is only when a little labour can procure abundance. On
this account a rich nation, when its manufactures are greatly
improven, may have an advantage over a poor one by underselling
it. The cotton and other commodities from China would undersell

any made with us, were it not for the long carriage, and other taxes that are laid upon them. We must not judge of the dearness of labour by the money or coin that is paid for it. One penny in some places will purchase as much as eighteen pence in others. In the country of the Mogul, where the day's wages are only two pence, labour is better rewarded than in some of our sugar islands where men are almost starving with four or five shillings a day. Coin therefore can be no proper estimate. Further, though human labour be employed both in the multiplication of commodities and of money, yet the chance of success is not equal. A farmer, by the proper cultivation of an acre, is sure of increase; but the miner may work again and again without success. Commodities must therefore multiply in greater proportion than gold and silver.

But again, the quantity of work which is done by the division of labour is much increased by the three following articles: first, increase of dexterity; secondly, the saving of time lost in passing from one species of labour to another; and thirdly, the invention of machinery. Of these in order:

First, when any kind of labour is reduced to a simple operation a frequency of action insensibly fits men to a dexterity in accomplishing it. A country smith not accustomed to make nails will work very hard for three or four hundred a day, and those, too, very bad; but a boy used to it will easily make two thousand, and those incomparably better; yet the improvement of dexterity in this very complex manufacture can never be equal to that in others. A nail-maker changes postures, blows the bellows, changes tools, etc., and therefore the quantity produced cannot be so great as in manufactures of pins and buttons, where the work is reduced to simple operations.

Secondly, there is always some time lost in passing from one species of labour to another, even when they are pretty much connected. When a person has been reading he must rest a little before he begins to write. This is still more the case with the country weaver, who is possessed of a little farm; he must saunter a little when he goes from one to the other. This in general is the case with the country labourers, they are always the greatest saunterers; the country employments of sowing, reaping, threshing being so different, they naturally acquire a habit of indolence, and are seldom very dexterous. By fixing every man to his own operation and preventing the shifting from one piece of labour to another, the quantity of work must be greatly increased.

Thirdly, the quantity of work is greatly increased by the invention of machines. Two men and three horses will do more in a day with the plough than twenty men without it. The miller and his servant will do more with the water miln than a dozen with the hand miln, though it too be a machine. The division of labour no doubt first gave occasion to the invention of machines. If a man's business in life is the performance of two or three things the bent of his mind will be to find out the cleverest way of doing it; but when the force of his mind is divided it cannot be expected that he should be so successful. We have not, nor cannot have, any complete history of the invention of machines because most of them are at first imperfect and receive gradual improvements and increase of powers from those who use them. It was probably a farmer who made the original plough though the improvements might be owing to some other. Some miserable slave who had perhaps been employed for a long time in grinding corn between two stones probably first found out the method of supporting the upper stone by a spindle. A miln-wright perhaps found out the way of turning the spindle with the hand, but he who contrived that the outer wheel should go by water was a philosopher whose business it is to do nothing but observe every-thing. They must have extensive views of things, who, as in this case, bring in the assistance of new powers not formerly applied. Whether he was an artisan or whatever he was who first executed this, he must have been a philosopher. Fire machines, wind and water-milns were the invention of philosophers, whose dexterity, too, is increased by a division of labour. They all divide themselves according to the different branches, into the mechanical, moral, political, chemical philosophers.

Thus we have shown how the quantity of labour is increased by machines.

5 *What gives Occasion to the Division of Labour*

We have already shown that the division of labour is the immediate cause of opulence; we shall next consider what gives occasion to the division of labour, or from what principles in our nature it can best be accounted for. We cannot imagine this to be an effect of human prudence. It was indeed made a law by Sesostris that every man should follow the employment of his father, but this is by no means suitable to the dispositions of human nature, and can never long take place; every one is fond of being a gentleman, be his father what he would. They who are strongest and, in the bustle of society, have got above the weak, must have as many under as to defend them in their station. From necessary causes, therefore, there must be as many in the lower stations as there is occasion for, there must be as many up as down, and no division can be over-stretched. But it is not this which gives occasion to the division of labour; it flows from a direct propensity in human nature for one man to barter with another, which is common to all men, and known to no other animal. Nobody ever saw a dog, the most sagacious animal, exchange a bone with his companion for another. Two greyhounds, indeed, in running down a hare, seem to have something like compact or agreement betwixt them, but this is nothing else but a concurrence of the same passions. If an animal intends to truck, as it were, or gain anything from man, it is by its fondness and kindness. Man, in the same manner, works on the self love of his fellows, by setting before them a sufficient tempta-tion to get what he wants. The language of this disposition is, 'Give me what I want, and you shall have what you want.' It is not from benevolence, as the dogs, but from self love that man expects anything. The brewer and the baker serve us not from benevolence, but from self love. No man but a beggar depends on benevolence, and even they would die in a week were their entire dependence upon it.

By this disposition to barter and exchange the surplus of one's labour for that of other people, in a nation of hunters, if any one has a talent for making bows and arrows better than his neigh-bours, he will at first make presents of them, and in return get presents of their game. By continuing this practice he will live better than before, and will have no occasion to provide for himself as the surplus of his own labour does it more effectually.

This disposition to barter is by no means founded upon different genius and talents. It is doubtful if there be any such difference at all, at least it is far less than we are aware of. Genius is more the effect of the division of labour than the latter is of it. The difference between a porter and a philosopher in the first four or five years of their life is, properly speaking, none at all. When they come to be employed in different occupations, their views widen and differ by degrees. As every one has this natural disposition to truck and barter, by which he provides for himself, there is no need for such different endowments; and accordingly, among savages there is always the greatest uniformity of character. In other animals of the same species we find a much greater difference than betwixt the philosopher and porter, antecedent to custom. The mastiff and spaniel have quite different powers, but though these animals are possessed of talents they cannot, as it were, bring them into the common stock and exchange their productions, and therefore their different talents are of no use to them. It is quite otherwise among mankind; they can exchange their several productions according to their quantity or quality; the philosopher and the porter are both of advantage to each other. The porter is of use in carrying burdens for the philosopher, and in his turn he burns his coals cheaper by the philosopher's invention of the fire machine.

Thus we have shown that different genius is not the foundation of this disposition to barter which is the cause of the division of labour. The real foundation of it is that principle to persuade which so much prevails in human nature. When any arguments are offered to persuade, it is always expected that they should have their proper effect. If a person asserts anything about the moon, though it should not be true, he will feel a kind of uneasiness in being contradicted, and would be very glad that the person he is endeavouring to persuade should be of the same way of thinking with himself. We ought then mainly to cultivate the power of persuasion, and indeed we do so without intending it. Since a whole life is spent in the exercise of it, a ready method of bargaining with each other must undoubtedly be attained. As was before observed, no animal can do this but by gaining the favour of those whom they would persuade. Sometimes, indeed, animals seem to act in concert, but there never is anything like bargain among them. Monkeys, when they rob a garden, throw the fruit from one to another, till they deposit it in the hoard, but there is always a scramble about the division of the booty, and usually some of them are killed.

6 *That the Division of Labour must be proportioned to the Extent of Commerce*

From all that has been said we may observe that the division of labour must always be proportioned to the extent of commerce. If ten people only want a certain commodity, the manufacture of it will never be so divided as if a thousand wanted it. Again, the division of labour in order to opulence, becomes always more perfect by the easy method of conveyance in a country. If the road be infested with robbers, if it be deep and conveyance not easy, the progress of commerce must be stopped. Since the mending of roads in England forty or fifty years ago its opulence has increased extremely. Water carriage is another convenience, as by it 300 ton can be conveyed at the expense of the tear and wear of the vessel, and the wages of five or six men, and that too in a shorter time than by a hundred wagons which will take six horses and a man each. Thus the division of labour is the great cause of the increase of public opulence, which is always proportioned to the industry of the people, and not to the quantity of gold and silver, as is foolishly imagined, and the industry of the people is always proportioned to the division of labour.

Having thus shown what gives occasion to public opulence, in farther considering this subject we propose to consider:

First, what circumstances regulate the price of commodities;

Secondly, money in two different views, first as the measure of value, and then as the instrument of commerce;

Thirdly, the history of commerce, in which shall be taken notice of the causes of the slow progress of opulence, both in ancient and modern times, which causes shall be shown either to affect agriculture or arts and manufactures;

Lastly, the effects of a commercial spirit, on the government, temper, and manners of a people, whether good or bad, and the proper remedies. Of these in order.

7 *What Circumstances regulate the Price of Commodities*

Of every commodity there are two different prices, which though apparently independent, will be found to have a necessary connexion, *viz.* the natural price and the market price. Both of these are regulated by certain circumstances. When men are induced to a certain species of industry, rather than any other, they must make as much by the employment as will maintain them while they are employed. An arrow-maker must be sure to exchange as much surplus product as will maintain him during as long time as he took to make them. But upon this principle in the different trades there must be a considerable difference, because some trades, such as those of the tailor and weaver, are not learned by casual observation and a little experience, like that of the day-labourer, but take a great deal of time and pains before they are acquired. When a person begins them, for a considerable time his work is of no use to his master or any other person, and therefore his master must be compensated, both for what maintains him and for what he spoils. When he comes to exercise his trade, he must be repaid what he has laid out, both of expenses and of apprentice fee, and as his life is not worth above ten or twelve years' purchase at most his wages must be high on account of the risk he runs of not having the whole made up. But again there are many arts which require more extensive knowledge than is to be got during the time of an apprenticeship. A blacksmith and weaver may learn their business well enough without any previous knowledge of mathematics, but a watchmaker must be acquainted with several sciences in order to undertake his business well, such as arithmetic, geometry, and astronomy with regard to the equation of time, and their wages must be high in order to compensate the additional expense. In general, this is the case in all the liberal arts, because after they have spent a long time in their education, it is ten to one if ever they make anything by it. Their wages therefore must be higher in proportion to the expense they have been at, the risk of not living long enough. and the risk of not having dexterity enough to manage their business. Among the lawyers there is not one among twenty that attains such knowledge and dexterity in his business as enables him to get back the expenses of his education, and many of them never make the price of their gown, as we say. The fees of lawyers are so far from being extravagant, as they are generally thought, that they are rather low in proportion. It is the eminence of the profession and not the money made by it that is the temptation for applying to it, and the dignity of that rank is to be considered as a part of what is made by it.

In the same manner we shall find that the price of gold and silver is not extravagant, if we consider it in this view for in a gold or silver mine there is a great chance of missing it altogether. If we suppose an equal number of men employed in raising corn and digging silver, the former will make more than the latter, because perhaps of forty or fifty employed in a mine, only twenty make anything at all. Some of the rest may indeed make fortunes, but every corn man succeeds in his undertakings so that upon the whole there is more made this way than the other. It is the ideal acquisition which is the principal temptation in a mine.

A man then has the natural price of his labour, when it is sufficient to maintain him during the time of labour, to defray the expense of education and to compensate the risk of not living long enough and of not succeeding in the business. When a man has this, there is sufficient encouragement to the labourer, and the commodity will be cultivated in proportion to the demand.

The market price of goods is regulated by quite other circumstances. When a buyer comes to the market, he never asks of the seller what expenses he has been at in producing them. The regulation of the market price of goods depends on the three following articles:

First, the demand, or need for the commodity. There is no demand for a thing of little use; it is not a rational object of desire.

Secondly, the abundance or scarcity of the commodity in proportion to the need of it. If the commodity be scarce, the price is raised, but if the quantity be more than is sufficient to supply the demand, the price falls. Thus it is that diamonds and other precious stones are dear, while iron, which is much more useful, is so many times cheaper, though this depends principally on the last cause, viz.:

Thirdly, the riches or poverty of those who demand. When there is not enough produced to serve everybody, the fortune of the bidders is the only regulation of the price. The story which is told of the merchant and the carrier in the deserts of Arabia is an evidence of this. The merchant gave 10,000 ducats for a certain quantity of water. His fortune here regulated the price, for if he had not had them, he could not have given them and if his fortune had been less, the water would have been cheaper. When the commodity is scarce, the seller must be content with that degree of wealth which they have who buy it. The case is much the same as in an auction. If two persons have an equal fondness for a book, he whose fortune is largest will carry it. Hence things that are very rare go always to rich countries. The King of France only could purchase that large diamond of so many thousand pounds value. Upon this principle, everything is dearer or cheaper according as it is the purchase of a higher or lower set of people. Utensils of gold are comeatable only by persons in certain circumstances. Those of silver fall to another set of people, and their prices are regulated by what the majority can give. The prices of corn and beer are regulated by what all the world can give, and on this account the wages of the day-labourer have a great influence upon the price of corn. When the price of corn rises, wages rise also, and *vice versa*; when the quantity of corn falls short, as in a sea-voyage, it always occasions a famine, and then the price becomes enormous. Corn then becomes the purchase of a higher set of people, and the lower must live on turnips and potatoes.

Thus we have considered the two prices, the natural and the market price, which every commodity is supposed to have. We observed before that however seemingly independent they appear to be, they are necessarily connected. This will appear from the following considerations. If the market price of any commodity is very great and the labour very highly rewarded, the market is prodigiously crowded with it, greater quantities of it are produced and it can be sold to the inferior ranks of people. If for every ten diamonds there were ten thousand, they would become the purchase of everybody, because they would become very cheap, and would sink to their natural price. Again when the market is over-stocked and there is not enough got for the labour of the manufacture nobody will bind to it, they cannot have a subsistence by it, because the market price falls then below the natural price. It is alleged that as the price of corn sink[s], the wages of the labourer should sink, as he is then better rewarded. It is true that if provisions were long cheap, as more people would flock to this labour where the wages are high, through this concurrence of labour the wages would come down, but we find that when the price of corn is doubled, the wages continue the same as before, because the labourers have no other way to turn themselves. The same is the case with menial servants.

From the above we may observe that whatever police tends to raise the market price above the natural, tends to diminish public opulence. Dearness and scarcity are in effect the same thing. When commodities are in abundance, they can be sold to the inferior ranks of people, who can afford to give less for them, but not if they are scarce. So far, therefore, as goods are a conveniency to the society, the society lives less happy when only the few can possess them. Whatever therefore keeps goods above their natural price for a permanency, diminishes [a] nation's opulence. Such are:

First, all taxes upon industry, upon leather, and upon shoes, which people grudge most, upon salt, beer, or whatever is the strong drink of the country, for no country wants some kind of it. Man is an anxious animal, and must have his care swept off by something that can exhilarate the spirits. It is alleged that this tax upon beer is an artificial security against drunkenness, but if we attend to it, [we will find] that it by no means prevents it. In countries where strong liquors are cheap as in France and Spain, the people are generally sober, but in northern countries, where they are dear, they do not get drunk with beer, but with spirituous liquors; nobody presses his friend to a glass of beer, unless he choose it.

Secondly, monopolies also destroy public opulence. The price of the monopolized goods is raised above what is sufficient for encouraging the labour. When only a certain person or persons have the liberty of importing a commodity, there is less of it imported than would otherwise be; the price of it is therefore higher, and fewer people supported by it. It is the concurrence of different labourers which always brings down the price. In monopolies, such as the Hudson's Bay and East India companies, the people engaged in them make the price what they please.

Thirdly, exclusive privileges of corporations have the same effect. The butchers and bakers raise the price of their goods as they please, because none but their own corporation is allowed to sell in the market, and therefore their meat must be taken, whether good or not. On this account there is always required a magistrate to fix the prices. For any free commodity, such as broad cloth, there is no occasion for this, but it is necessary with bakers, who may agree among themselves to make the quantity and price what they please. Even a magistrate is not a good enough expedient for this, as he must always settle the price at the outside, else the remedy must be worse than the disease, for nobody would apply to these businesses, and a famine would ensue. On this account bakers and brewers have always profitable trades.

As what raises the market price above the natural one diminishes public opulence, so what brings it down below it has the same effect.

It is only upon manufactures to be exported that this can usually be done by any law or regulation, such as the bounty allowed by the government upon coarse linen, by which it becomes exportable, when under twelve pence a yard. The public paying a great part of the price, it can be sold cheaper to foreigners than what is sufficient for encouraging the labour. In the same manner, by the bounty of five shillings upon the quarter of corn when sold under forty shillings, as the public pays an eighth part of the price, it can be sold just so much cheaper at a foreign market. By this bounty the commodity is rendered more comeatable, and a greater quantity of it produced, but then it breaks what may be called the natural balance of industry. The disposition to apply to the production of that commodity is not proportioned to the natural cause of the demand, but to both that and the annexed bounty. It has not only this effect with regard to the particular commodity, but likewise people are called from other productions which are less encouraged, and thus the balance of industry is broken.

Again, after the ages of hunting and fishing, in which provisions were the immediate produce of their labour, when manufactures were introduced, nothing could be produced without a great deal of time. It was a long time before the weaver could carry to the market the cloth which he bought in flax. Every trade therefore requires a stock of food, clothes, and lodging to carry it on. Suppose then, as is really the case in every country, that there is in store a stock of food, clothes, and lodging, the number of people that are employed must be in proportion to it. If the price of one commodity is sunk below its natural price, while another is above it, there is a smaller quantity of the stored stock left to support the whole. On account of the natural connexion of all trades in the stock, by allowing bounties to one you take away the stock from the rest. This has been the real consequence of the corn bounty.

The price of corn being sunk, the rent of the farms sinks also, yet the bounty upon corn, which was laid on at the time of the taxes, was intended to raise the rent, and had the effect for some time, because the tenants were assured of a price for their corn, both at home and abroad. But though the effects of the bounty encouraging agriculture brought down the price of corn, yet it raised the grass farms, for the more corn the less grass. The price of grass being raised, butchers' meat, in consequence of its dependence upon it, must be raised also, so that if the price of corn is diminished, the price of other commodities is necessarily raised. The price of corn has indeed fallen from forty-two to thirty-five, but the price of hay has risen from twenty-five to near fifty shillings. As the price of hay has risen, horses are not so easily kept, and therefore the price of carriage has risen also. But whatever increases the price of carriage, diminishes plenty in the market. Upon the whole, therefore, it is by far the best police to leave things to their natural course, and allow no bounties, nor impose taxes on commodities.

Thus we have shown what circumstances regulate the price of commodities, which was the first thing proposed.

Three:

Two Writings by David Ricardo

We publish here the entire text of Ricardo's *An Essay on the Influence of a Low Price of Corn on the Profit of Stock*, and also the unfinished (later version) of his paper '*Absolute Value and Exchangeable Value*' (see pp. 180–191 ff.). '*Absolute Value and Exchangeable Value*' remained unpublished until included in Volume IV of *The Works and Correspondence of David Ricardo* edited by Piero Sraffa (Cambridge University Press, 1951), which volume also includes *An Essay on the Low Price of Corn*. The *Essay* puts forward the theory of the determination of the rate of profit in terms of corn. *Absolute Value and Exchangeable Value* (which was written just before Ricardo's death) shows the difficulties which Ricardo always encountered in the definition of a 'perfect measure of value' within the ambit of a labour theory of value; Sraffa's 'Introduction' to the *Works* is fundamental to an appreciation of the questions involved in this respect.

Introduction

In treating on the subject of the profits of capital, it is necessary to consider the principles which regulate the rise and fall of rent; as rent and profits, it will be seen, have a very intimate connexion with each other. The principles which regulate rent are briefly stated in the following pages, and differ in a very slight degree from those which have been so fully and so ably developed by Mr. Malthus in his late excellent publication, to which I am very much indebted. The consideration of those principles, together with those which regulate the profit of stock, have convinced me of the policy of leaving the importation of corn unrestricted by law. From the general principle set forth in all Mr. Malthus's publications, I am persuaded that he holds the same opinion as far as profit and wealth are concerned with the question;—but, viewing, as he does, the danger as formidable of depending on foreign supply for a large portion of our food, he considers it wise, on the whole, to restrict importation. Not participating with him in those fears, and perhaps estimating the advantages of a cheap price of corn at a higher value, I have come to a different conclusion. Some of the objections urged in his last publication, *Grounds of an Opinion*, etc. I have endeavoured to answer; they appear to me to be unconnected with the political danger he apprehends, and to be inconsistent with the general doctrines of the advantages of a free trade, which he has himself, by his writings, so ably contributed to establish.

An Essay on the Influence of a Low price of Corn on the Profit of Stock

Mr. Malthus very correctly defines, 'the rent of land to be that portion of the value of the whole produce which remains to the owner, after all the outgoings belonging to its cultivation, of whatever kind, have been paid, including the profits of the capital employed, estimated according to the usual and ordinary rate of the profits of agricultural stodk at the time being'.

Whenever, then, the usual and ordinary rate of the profits of agricultural stock, and all the outgoings belonging to the cultivation of land, are together equal to the value of the whole produce, there can be no rent.

And when the whole produce is only equal in value to the outgoings necessary to cultivation, there can neither be rent nor profit.

In the first settling of a country rich in fertile land, and which may be had by any one who chooses to take it, the whole produce, after deducting the outgoings belonging to cultivation, will be the profits of capital, and will belong to the owner of such capital, without any deduction whatever for rent.

Thus, if the capital employed by an individual on such land were of the value of two hundred quarters of wheat, of which half consisted of fixed capital, such as buildings, implements, etc. and the other half of circulating capital,—if, after replacing the fixed and circulating capital, the value of the remaining produce were one hundred quarters of wheat, or of equal value with one hundred quarters of wheat, the neat profit to the owner of capital would be 50 per cent. or one hundred profit on two hundred capital.

For a period of some duration, the profits of agricultural stock might continue at the same rate, because land equally fertile, and equally well situated, might be abundant, and therefore, might be cultivated on the same advantageous terms, in proportion as the capital of the first and subsequent settlers augmented.

Profits might even increase because, the population increasing at a more rapid rate than capital, wages might fall; and instead of the value of one hundred quarters of wheat being necessary for the circulating capital, ninety only might be required: in which case, the profits of stock would rise from 50 to 57 per cent.

Profits might also increase, because improvements might take place in agriculture, or in the implements of husbandry, which would augment the produce with the same cost of production.

If wages rose, or a worse system of agriculture were practised, profits would again fall.

These are circumstances which are more or less at all times in operation—they may retard or accelerate the natural effects of the progress of wealth, by raising or lowering profits—by increasing or diminishing the supply of food, with the employment of the same capital on the land.[1]

We will, however, suppose that no improvements take place in agriculture, and that capital and population advance in the proper proportion, so that the real wages of labour, continue uniformly the same;—that we may know what peculiar effects are to be ascribed to the growth of capital, the increase of population, and the extension of cultivation, to the more remote, and less fertile land.

In this state of society, when the profits on agricultural stock, by the supposition, are 50 per cent. the profits on all other capital, employed either in the rude manufactures, common to such a stage of society, or in foreign commerce, as the means of procuring in exchange for raw produce, those commodities which may be in demand, will be also, 50 per cent.[2]

If the profits on capital employed in trade were more than 50 per cent. capital would be withdrawn from the land to be employed in trade. If they were less, capital would be taken from trade to agriculture.

After all the fertile land in the immediate neighbourhood of the first settlers were cultivated, if capital and population increased, more food would be required, and it could only be procured from land not so advantageously situated. Supposing then the land to be equally fertile, the necessity of employing more labourers, horses, etc. to carry the produce from the place where it was grown, to the place where it was to be consumed, although no alteration were to take place in the wages of labour, would make it necessary that more capital should be permanently employed to obtain the same produce. Suppose this addition to be of the value of ten quarters of wheat, the whole capital employed on the new land would be two hundred and ten, to obtain the same return as on the old; and, consequently the profits of stock would fall from 50 to 43 per cent. or ninety on two hundred and ten.[3]

On the land first cultivated, the return would be the same as before, namely, 50 per cent. or one hundred quarters of wheat; but, the general profits of stock being regulated by the profits made on the least profitable employment of capital on agriculture, a division of the one hundred quarters would take place, 43 per cent. or eighty-six quarters would constitute the profit of stock, and 7 per cent. or fourteen quarters, would constitute rent. And that such a division must take place is evident, when we consider that the owner of the capital of the value of two hundred and ten quarters of wheat would obtain precisely the same profit, whether he cultivated the distant land, or paid the first settler fourteen quarters for rent.

In this stage, the profits on all capital employed in trade would fall to 43 per cent.

If, in the further progress of population and wealth, the produce of more land were required to obtain the same return, it might be necessary to employ, either on account of distance, or the worse quality of land, the value of two hundred and twenty quarters of wheat, the profits of stock would then fall to 36 per cent. or eighty on two hundred and twenty, and the rent of the first land would rise to twenty-eight quarters of wheat, and on the second portion of land cultivated, rent would now commence, and would amount to fourteen quarters.

The profits on all trading capital would also fall to 36 per cent.

Thus by bringing successively land of a worse quality, or less favourably situated into cultivation, rent would rise on the land previously cultivated, and precisely in the same degree would profits fall; and if the smallness of profits do not check accumulation, there are hardly any limits to the rise of rent, and the fall of profit.

If instead of employing capital at a distance on new land, an additional capital of the value of two hundred and ten quarters of wheat be employed on the first land cultivated, and its return were in like manner 43 per cent. or ninety on two hundred and ten; the produce of 50 per cent. on the first capital, would be divided in the same manner as before 43 per cent. or eighty-six quarters would constitute profit, and fourteen quarters rent.

If two hundred and twenty quarters were employed in addition with the same result as before, the first capital would afford a rent of twenty-eight; and the second of fourteen quarters; and the profits on the whole capital of six hundred and thirty quarters would be equal, and would amount to 36 per cent.

Supposing that the nature of man was so altered, that he required double the quantity of food that is now necessary for his subsistence, and consequently, that the expenses of cultivation were very greatly increased. Under such circumstances the knowledge and capital of an old society employed on fresh and fertile land in a new country would leave a much less surplus produce; consequently, the profits of stock could never be so high. But accumulation, though slower in its progress, might still go on, and rent would begin just as before, when more distant or less fertile land were cultivated.

The natural limit to population would of course be much earlier, and rent could never rise to the height to which it may now do; because, in the nature of things, land of the same poor quality would never be brought into cultivation—nor could the same amount of capital be employed on the better land with any adequate return of profit.[4]

The following table is constructed on the supposition that the first portion of land yields one hundred quarters profit on a capital of two hundred quarters; the second portion, ninety quarters on two hundred and ten, according to the foregoing

TABLE, *showing the Progress of Rent and Profit under*

Capital estimated in quarters of wheat	Profit per cent	Neat produce in quarters of wheat after paying the cost of production on each capital	Profit of 1st portion of land in quarters of wheat	Rent of 1st portion of land in quarters of wheat	Profit of 2nd portion of land in quarters of wheat	Rent of 2nd portion of land in quarters of wheat	Profit of 3rd portion of land in quarters of wheat	Rent of 3rd portion of land in quarters of wheat
200	50	100	100	none				
210	43	90	86	14	90	none		
220	36	80	72	28	76	14	80	none
230	30	70	60	40	63	27	66	14
240	25	60	50	50	52½	37½	55	25
250	20	50	40	60	42	48	44	36
260	15	40	30	70	31½	58½	33	47
270	11	30	22	78	23	67	24	56

When the whole capital employed is		Whole amount of rent received by landlords in quarters of wheat	Whole amount of profits in quarters received by owners of stock	Profit per cent on the whole capital	Rent per cent on the whole capital	Total produce in quarters of wheat, after paying the cost of production
1st Period	200	none	100	50		100
2nd Period	410	14	176	43	3½	190
3rd Period	630	42	228	36	6½	270
4th Period	860	81	259	30	9½	340
5th Period	1100	125	275	25	11½	400
6th Period	1350	180	270	20	13½	450
7th Period	1610	248½	241½	15	15½	490
8th Period	1880	314½	205½	11	16½	520

calculations.[5] It will be seen that during the progress of a country the whole produce raised on its land will increase, and for a certain time that part of the produce which belongs to the profits of stock, as well as that part which belongs to rent will increase; but that at a later period, every accumulation of capital will be attended with an absolute, as well as a proportionate diminution of profits,—though rents will uniformly increase. A less revenue, it will be seen, will be enjoyed by the owner of stock, when one thousand three hundred and fifty quarters are employed on the different qualities of land, than when one thousand one hundred were employed. In the former case the whole profits will be only two hundred and seventy, in the latter two hundred and seventy-five; and when one thousand six hundred and ten are employed, profits will fall to two hundred and forty-one and a half.[6]

n assumed Augmentation of Capital

Profit of 4th portion of land in quarters of wheat	Rent of 4th portion of land in quarters of wheat	Profit of 5th portion of land in quarters of wheat	Rent of 5th portion of land in quarters of wheat	Profit of 6th portion of land in quarters of wheat	Rent of 6th portion of land in quarters of wheat	Profit of 7th portion of land in quarters of wheat	Rent of 7th portion of land in quarters of wheat	Profit of 8th portion of land in quarters of wheat
0	none							
7½	12½	60	none					
6	24	48	12	50	none			
4½	35½	36	24	37½	12½	40	none	
5·3	44·7	26·4	33·6	27½	22½	27·6	12·4	29·7

This is a view of the effects of accumulation which is exceedingly curious, and has, I believe, never before been noticed.

It will be seen by the table, that, in a progressive country, rent is not only absolutely increasing, but that it is also increasing in its ratio to the capital employed on the land; thus when four hundred and ten was the whole capital employed, the landlord obtained 3¼ per cent.; when one thousand one hundred—13¼ per cent.; and when one thousand eight hundred and eighty—16½ per cent. The landlord not only obtains a greater produce, but a larger share.

Rent[7] then is in all cases a portion of the profits previously obtained on the land. It is never a new creation of revenue, but always part of a revenue already created.

Profits of stock fall only, because land equally well adapted to produce food cannot be procured; and the degree of the fall of profits, and the rise of rents, depends wholly on the increased expense of production.

If, therefore, in the progress of countries in wealth and population, new portions of fertile land could be added to such countries, with every increase of capital, profits would never fall, nor rents rise.[8]

If the money price of corn, and the wages of labour, did not vary in price in the least degree, during the progress of the country in wealth and population, still profits would fall and rents would rise; because more labourers would be employed on the more distant or less fertile land, in order to obtain the same supply of raw produce; and therefore the cost of production would have increased, whilst the value of the produce continued the same.

But the price of corn, and of all other raw produce, has been invariably observed to rise as a nation became wealthy, and was obliged to have recourse to poorer lands for the production of part of its food; and very little consideration will convince us that such is the effect which would naturally be expected to take place under such circumstances.

The exchangeable value of all commodities, rises as the difficulties of their production increase. If then new difficulties occur in the production of corn, from more labour being necessary, whilst no more labour is required to produce gold, silver, cloth, linen, etc., the exchangeable value of corn will necessarily rise, as compared with those things. On the contrary, facilities in the production of corn, or of any other commodity of whatever kind, which shall afford the same produce with less labour, will lower its exchangeable value.[9] Thus we see that improvements in agriculture, or in the implements of husbandry, lower the exchangeable value of corn;[10] improvements in the machinery connected with the manufacture of cotton, lower the exchangeable value of cotton goods; and improvements in mining, or the discovery of new and more abundant mines of the precious metals, lower the value of gold and silver, or which is the same thing, raises the price of all other commodities. Wherever competition can have its full effect, and the production of the commodity be not limited by nature, as in the case with some wines, the difficulty or facility of their production will ultimately regulate their exchangeable value.[11] The sole effect then of the progress of wealth on prices, independently of all improvements, either in agriculture or manufactures, appears to be to raise the price of raw produce and of labour, leaving all other commodities at their original prices, and to lower general profits in consequence of the general rise of wages.

This fact is of more importance than at first sight appears, as it relates to the interest of the landlord, and the other parts of the community. Not only is the situation of the landlord improved, (by the increasing difficulty of procuring food, in consequence of accumulation) by obtaining an increased quantity of the produce of the land, but also by the increased exchangeable value of that quantity. If his rent be increased from fourteen to twenty-eight quarters, it would be more than doubled, because he would be able to command more than double the quantity of commodities, in exchange for the twenty-eight quarters. As rents are agreed for, and paid in money, he would, under the circumstances supposed, receive more than double of his former money rent.

In like manner, if rent fell, the landlord would suffer two losses; he would be a loser of that portion of the raw produce which constituted his additional rent; and further, he would be a loser by the depreciation in the real or exchangeable value of the raw produce in which, or in the value of which, his remaining rent would be paid.[12]

As the revenue of the farmer is realized in raw produce, or in the value of raw produce, he is interested, as well as the landlod, in its high exchangeable value, but a low price of produce may be compensated to him by a great additional quantity.

It follows then, that the interest of the landlord is always opposed to the interest of every other class in the community. His situation is never so prosperous, as when food is scarce and dear: whereas, all other persons are greatly benefited by procuring food cheap. High rent and low profits, for they invariably accompany each other, ought never to be the subject of complaint, if they are the effect of the natural course of things.

They are the most unequivocal proofs of wealth and prosperity, and of an abundant population, compared with the fertility of the soil. The general profits of stock depend wholly on the profits of the last portion of capital employed on the land; if, therefore, landlords were to relinquish the whole of their rents, they would neither raise the general profits of stock, nor lower the price of corn to the consumer. It would have no other effect, as Mr. Malthus has observed, than to enable those farmers, whose lands now pay a rent, to live like gentlemen, and they would have to expend that portion of the general revenue which now falls to the share of the landlord.

A nation is rich, not according to the abundance of its money, nor to the high money value at which its commodities circulate, but according to the abundance of its commodities, contributing to its comforts and enjoyments. Although this is a proposition, from which few would dissent, many look with the greatest alarm at the prospect of the diminution of their money revenue, though such reduced revenue should have so improved in exchangeable value, as to procure considerably more of all the necessaries and luxuries of life.

If then, the principles here stated as governing rent and profit be correct, general profits on capital can only be raised by a fall in the exchangeable value of food, and which fall can only arise from three causes:

1st. The fall of the real wages of labour, which shall enable the farmer to bring a greater excess of produce to market.

2d. Improvements in agriculture, or in the implements of husbandry, which shall also increase the excess of produce.

3dly. The discovery of new markets, from whence corn may be imported at a cheaper price than it can be grown for at home.

The first of these causes is more or less permanent, according as the price from which wages fall, is more or less near that remuneration for labour, which is necessary to the actual subsistence of the labourer.

The rise or fall of wages is common to all states of society, whether it be the stationary, the advancing, or the retrograde state. In the stationary state, it is regulated wholly by the increase or falling off of the population. In the advancing state, it depends on whether the capital or the population advance, at the more rapid course. In the retrograde state, it depends on whether population or capital decrease with the greater rapidity.

As experience demonstrates that capital and population alternately take the lead, and wages in consequence are liberal or scanty, nothing can be positively laid down, respecting profits, as far as wages are concerned.

But I think it may be most satisfactorily proved, that in every society advancing in wealth and population, independently of the effect produced by liberal or scanty wages, general profits must fall, unless there be improvements in agriculture, or corn can be imported at a cheaper price.

It seems the necessary result of the principles which have been stated to regulate the progress of rent.

This principle will, however, not be readily admitted by those who ascribe to the extension for commerce, and discovery of new markets, where our commodities can be sold dearer, and foreign commodities can be bought cheaper, the progress of profits, without any reference whatever to the state of the land, and the rate of profit obtained on the last portions of capital employed upon it. Nothing is more common than to hear it asserted, that profits on agriculture no more regulate the profits of commerce, than that the profits of commerce regulate the profits on agriculture. It is contended, that they alternately take the lead; and, if the profits of commerce rise, which it is said they do, when new markets are discovered, the profits of agriculture will also rise; for it is admitted, that if they did not do so, capital would be withdrawn from the land to be employed in the more profitable trade. But if the principles respecting the progress of rent be correct, it is evident, that with the same population and capital, whilst none of the agricultural capital is withdrawn from the cultivation of the land, agricultural profits cannot rise, nor can rent fall: either then it must be contended, which is at variance with all the principles of political economy, that the profits on commercial capital will rise considerably, whilst the profits on agricultural capital suffer no alteration, or, that under such circumstances, the profits on commerce will not rise.[13]

It is this latter opinion which I consider as the true one. I do not deny that the first discoverer of a new and better market may, for a time, before competition operates, obtain unusual profits. He may either sell the commodities he exports at a higher price than those who are ignorant of the new market, or he may purchase the commodities imported at a cheaper price. Whilst he, or a few more, exclusively follow this trade their profits will be above the level of general profits. But it is of the general rate of profit that we are speaking, and not of the profits of a few individuals; and I cannot doubt that, in proportion as such trade shall be generally known and followed, there will be such a fall in the price of the foreign commodity in the importing country, in consequence of its increased abundance, and the greater facility with which it is procured, that its sale will afford only the common rate of profits—that so far from the high profits obtained by the few who first engaged in the new trade elevating the general rate of profits—those profits will themselves sink to the ordinary level.

The effects are precisely similar to those which follow from the use of improved machinery at home.

Whilst the use of the machine is confined to one, or a very few manufacturers, they may obtain unusual profits, because they are enabled to sell their commodities at a price much above the cost of production—but as soon as the machine becomes general to the whole trade, the price of the commodities will sink to the actual cost of production, leaving only the usual and ordinary profits.

During the period of capital moving from one employment to another, the profits on that to which capital is flowing will be relatively high, but will continue so no longer than till the requisite capital is obtained.

There are two ways in which a country may be benefited by trade—one by the increase of the general rate of profits, which, according to my opinion, can never take place but in consequence of cheap food, which is beneficial only to those who derive a revenue from the employment of their capital, either as farmers, manufacturers, merchants, or capitalists, lending their money at interest—the other by the abundance of commodities, and by a fall in their exchangeable value, in which the whole community participate. In the first case, the revenue of the country is augmented—in the second the same revenue becomes efficient in procuring a greater amount of the necessaries and luxuries of life.

It is in this latter mode only [14] that nations are benefited by the extension of commerce, by the division of labour in manufactures, and by the discovery of machinery, they all augment the amount of commodities, and contribute very much to the ease and happiness of mankind; but, they have no effect on the rate of profits, because they do not augment the produce compared with the cost of production on the land, and it is impossible that all other profits should rise whilst the profits on land are either stationary, or retrograde.

Profits then depend on the price, or rather on the value of food. Every thing which gives facility to the production of food, however scarce, or however abundant commodities may become, will raise the rate of profits, whilst on the contrary, everything which shall augment the cost of production without augmenting the quantity of food,[15] will, under every circumstance, lower the general rates of profits. The facility of obtaining food is beneficial in two ways to the owners of capital, it at the same time raises profits and increases the amount of consumable commodities. The facility in obtaining all other things, only increases the amount of commodities.

If, then, the power of purchasing cheap food be of such great importance, and if the importation of corn will tend to reduce its price, arguments almost unanswerable respecting the danger of dependence on foreign countries for a portion of our food, for in no other view will the question bear an argument, ought to be brought forward to induce us to restrict importation, and thereby forcibly to detain capital in an employment which it would otherwise leave for one much more advantageous.

If the legislature were at once to adopt a decisive policy with regard to the trade in corn—if it were to allow a permanently free trade, and did not with every variation of price, alternately restrict and encourage importation, we should undoubtedly be a regularly importing country. We should be so in consequence of the superiority of our wealth and population, compared to the fertility of our soil over our neighbours. It is only when a country is comparatively wealthy, when all its fertile land is in a state of high cultivation, and that it is obliged to have recourse to its inferior lands to obtain the food necessary for its population; or when it is originally without the advantages of a fertile soil, that it can become profitable to import corn.[16]

It is, then, the dangers of dependence on foreign supply for any considerable quantity of our food, which can alone be opposed to the many advantages which, circumstanced as we are, would attend the importation of corn.

These dangers do not admit of being very correctly estimated, they are in some degree, matters of opinion and cannot like the advantages on the other side, be reduced to accurate calculation. They are generally stated to be two—1st, that in the case of war a combination of the continental powers, or the influence of our principal enemy, might deprive us of our accustomed supply—2dly, that when bad seasons occurred abroad the exporting countries would have, and would exercise, the power of withholding the quantity usually exported to make up for their own deficient supply.[17]

If we became a regularly importing country, and foreigners could confidently rely on the demand of our market, much more land would be cultivated in the corn countries with a view to exportation. When we consider the value of even a few weeks consumption of corn in England, no interruption could be given to the export trade, if the continent supplied us with any considerable quantity of corn, without the most extensively ruinous commercial distress—distress which no sovereign, or combination of sovereigns, would be willing to inflict on their people; and, if willing, it would be a measure to which probably no people would submit. It was the endeavour of Buonaparte to prevent the exportation of the raw produce of Russia, more than [any] other cause, which produced the astonishing efforts of the people of that country against the most powerful force perhaps ever assembled to subjugate a nation.

The immense capital which would be employed on the land, could not be withdrawn suddenly, and under such circumstances, without immense loss; besides which, the glut of corn in their markets, which would affect their whole supply, and lower its value beyond calculation; the failure of those returns, which are essential in all commercial adventures, would occasion a scene of wide spreading ruin, which if a country would patiently endure, would render it unfit to wage war with any prospect of success. We have all witnessed the distress in this country, and we have all heard of the still greater distress in Ireland, from a fall in the price of corn, at a time too when it is acknowledged that our own crop has been deficient; when importation has been regulated by price, and when we have not experienced any of the effects of a glut. Of what nature would that distress have been if the price of corn had fallen to a half a quarter, or an eighth part of the present price. For the effects of plenty or scarcity, in the price of corn are incalculably greater than in proportion to the increase or deficiency of quantity. These, then, are the inconveniencies which the exporting countries would have to endure.

Ours would not be light. A great diminution in our usual supply, amounting probably to one-eighth of our whole consumption, it must be confessed, would be an evil of considerable magnitude; but we have obtained a supply equal to this, even when the growth of foreign countries was not regulated by the constant demand of our market. We all know the prodigious effects of a high price in procuring a supply. It cannot, I think be doubted, that we should obtain a considerable quantity from those countries with which we were not at war; which, with the most economical use of our own produce, and the quantity in store,[18] would enable us to subsist till we had bestowed the necessary capital and labour on our own land with a view to future production. That this would be a most afflicting change, I certainly allow; but I am fully persuaded that we should not be driven to such an alternative, and that, notwithstanding the war, we should be freely supplied with the corn, expressly grown in foreign countries for our consumption. Buonaparte, when he was most hostile to us, permitted the exportation of corn to England by licences, when our prices were high from a bad harvest, even when all other commerce was prohibited. Such a state of things could not come upon us suddenly; a danger of this nature would be partly foreseen, and due precautions would be taken. Would it be wise then to legislate with the view of preventing an evil which might never occur; and, to ward off a most improbable danger, sacrifice annually a revenue of some millions?

In contemplating a trade in corn, unshackled by restrictions on importation, and a consequent supply from France, and other countries, where it can be brought to market, at a price not much above half that at which we can ourselves produce it on some of our poorer lands, Mr. Malthus does not sufficiently allow for the greater quantity of corn, which would be grown abroad, if importation was to become the settled policy of this country. There cannot be the least doubt that if the corn countries could depend on the markets of England for a regular demand, if they could be perfectly secure that our laws respecting the corn trade, would not be repeatedly vacillating between bounties, restrictions, and prohibitions, a much larger supply would be grown, and the danger of a greatly diminished exportation, in consequence of bad seasons, would be less likely to occur. Countries which have never yet supplied us might, if our policy was fixed, afford us a considerable quantity.

It is at such times that it would be particularly the interest of foreign countries to supply our wants, as the exchangeable value of corn does not rise in proportion only to the deficiency of supply, but two, three, four, times as much, according to the amount of the deficiency.

If the consumption of England is ten million quarters, which, in an average year, would sell for forty millions of money; and, if the supply should be deficient one fourth, the seven million five hundred thousand quarters would not sell for forty millions only, but probably for fifty millions, or more. Under the circumstances, then, of bad seasons, the exporting country would content itself with the smallest possible quantity necessary for their own consumption, and would take advantage of the high price in England, to sell all they could spare, as not only would corn be high, as compared with money, but as compared with all other things; and if the growers of corn adopted any other rule, they would be in a worse situation, as far as regarded wealth, than if they had constantly limited the growth of corn to the wants of their own people.

If one hundred millions of capital were employed on the land, to obtain the quantity necessary to their own subsistence, and twenty millions more, that they might export the produce, they would lose the whole return of the twenty millions in the scarce year, which they would not have done had they not been an exporting country.

At whatever price exportation might be restricted, by foreign countries, the chance of corn rising to that price would be diminished by the greater quantity produced in consequence of our demand.

With respect to the supply of corn, it has been remarked, in reference to a single country, that if the crops are bad in one district, they are generally productive in another; that if the weather is injurious to one soil, or to one situation, it is beneficial to a different soil and different situation; and, by this compensating power, Providence has bountifully secured us from the frequent recurrence of dearths. If this remark be just, as applied to one country, how much more strongly may it be applied to all the countries together which compose our world? Will not the deficiency of one country be made up by the plenty of another? and, after the experience which we have had of the power of high prices to procure a supply, can we have any just reason to fear that we shall be exposed to any particular danger from depending on importation, for so much corn as may be necessary for a few weeks of our consumption.

From all that I can learn, the price of corn in Holland, which country depends almost wholly on foreign supply, has been remarkably steady, even during the convulsed times which Europe has lately experienced—a convincing proof, notwithstanding the smallness of the country, that the effects of bad seasons are not exclusively borne by importing countries.

That great improvements have been made in agriculture, and that much capital has been expended on the land, it is not attempted to deny; but, with all those improvements, we have not overcome the natural impediments resulting from our increasing wealth and prosperity, which obliges us to cultivate at a disadvantage our poor lands, if the importation of corn is restricted or prohibited. If we were left to ourselves, unfettered by legislative enactments, we should gradually withdraw our capital from the cultivation of such lands, and import the produce which is at present raised upon them. The capital withdrawn would be employed in the manufacture of such commodities as would be exported in return for the corn.[19] Such a distribution of part of the capital of the country, would be more advantageous, or it would not be adopted. This principle is one of the best established in the science of political economy and by no one is more readily admitted than by Mr. Malthus. It is the foundation of all his arguments, in his comparison of the advantages and disadvantages attending an unrestricted trade in corn, in his 'Observations on the Corn Laws'.

In his last publication, however, in one part of it, he dwells with much stress on the losses of agricultural capital, which the country would sustain, by allowing an unrestricted importation. He laments the loss of that which by the course of events has become of no use to us, and by the employment of which we actually lose. We might just as fairly have been told, when the steam-engine, or Mr. Arkwright's cotton-machine was brought to perfection, that it would be wrong to adopt the use of them, because the value of the old clumsy machinery would be lost to us. That the farmers of the poorer lands would be losers, there can be no doubt, but the public would gain many times the amount of their losses; and, after the exchange of capital from land to manufactures had been effected, the farmers themselves, as well as every other class of the community, except the landholders, would very considerably increase their profits.

It might, however, be desirable, that the farmers, during their current leases, should be protected against the losses which they would undoubtedly suffer from the new value of money, which would result from a cheap price of corn, under their existing money engagements with their landlords.

Although the nation would sacrifice much more than the farmers would save even by a temporary high price of corn, it might be just to lay restrictive duties on importation for three or four years, and to declare that, after that period, the trade in corn should be free, and that imported corn should be subject to no other duty than such as we might find it expedient to impose on corn of our own growth.[20]

Mr. Malthus is, no doubt, correct, when he says, 'If merely the best modes of cultivation now in use, in some parts of Great Britain, were generally extended, and the whole country was brought to a level, in proportion to its natural advantages of soil and situation, by the further accumulation and more equable distribution of capital and skill, the quantity of additional produce would be immense, and would afford the means of subsistence to a very great increase of population.'[21]

This reflection is true, and is highly pleasing—it shows that we are yet at a great distance from the end of our resources, and that we may contemplate an increase of prosperity and wealth, far exceeding that of any country which has preceeded us. This may take place under either system, that of importation or restriction, though not with an equally accelerated pace, and is no argument why we should not, at every period of our improvement, avail ourselves of the full extent of the advantages offered to our acceptance —it is no reason why we should not make the very best disposition of our capital, so as to ensure the most abundant return. The land has, as I before said, been compared by Mr. Malthus to a great number of machines, all susceptible of continued improvement by the application of capital to them, but yet of very different original qualities and powers. Would it be wise at a great expense to use some of the worst of these machines, when at a less expense we could hire the very best from our neighbours.

Mr. Malthus thinks that a low money price of corn would not be

favourable to the lower classes of society, because the real exchangeable value of labour; that is, its power of commanding the
necessaries, conveniences, and luxuries of life, would not be augmented, but diminished by a low money price. Some of his
observations on this subject are certainly of great weight, but he
does not sufficiently allow for the effects of a better distribution of
the national capital on the situation of the lower classes. It would be
beneficial to them, because the same capital would employ more
hands; besides, that the greater profits would lead to further
accumulations; and thus would a stimulus be given to population
by really high wages, which could not fail for a long time to
ameliorate the condition of the labouring classes.

The effects on the interests of this class, would be nearly the
same as the effects of improved machinery, which, it is now no
longer questioned, has a decided tendency to raise the real wages
of labour.

Mr. Malthus also observes, 'that of the commercial and manufacturing classes, only those who are directly engaged in foreign
trade will feel the benefit of the importing system'.

If the view which has been taken of rent be correct,—if it rise
as general profits fall, and falls as general profits rise,—and if the
effect of importing corn is to lower rent, which has been admitted,
and ably exemplified by Mr. Malthus himself,—all who are concerned in trade,—all capitalists whatever, whether they be farmers,
manufacturers, or merchants, will have a great augmentation of
profits. A fall in the price of corn, in consequence of improvements
in agriculture or of importation, will lower the exchangeable value
of corn only,—the price of no other commodity will be affected. If,
then, the price of labour falls, which it must do when the price of
corn is lowered, the real profits of all descriptions must rise; and no
person will be so materially benefited as the manufacturing and
commercial part of society.

If the demand for home commodities should be diminished,
because of the fall of rent on the part of the landlords, it will be
increased in a far greater degree by the increased opulence of the
commercial classes.

If restrictions on the importation of corn should take place, I do
not apprehend, that we shall lose any part of our foreign trade; on
this point, I agree with Mr. Malthus. In the case of a free trade in

corn, it would be considerably augmented; but the question is not, whether we can retain the same foreign trade,—but, whether, in both cases, it will be equally profitable.

Our commodities would not sell abroad for more or for less in consequence of a free trade, and a cheap price of corn; but the cost of production to our manufacturers would be very different if the price of corn was eighty, or was sixty shillings per quarter; and consequently profits would be augmented by all the cost saved in the production of the exported commodities.

Mr. Malthus notices an observation, which was first made by Hume, that a rise of prices, has a magic effect on industry: he states the effects of a fall to be proportionally depressing.[22] A rise of prices has been stated to be one of the advantages, to counterbalance the many evils attendant on a depreciation of money, from a real fall in the value of the precious metals, from raising the denomination of the coin, or from the over-issue of paper money.

It is said to be beneficial, because it betters the situation of the commercial classes at the expense of those enjoying fixed incomes;—and that it is chiefly in those classes, that the great accumulations are made, and productive industry encouraged.

A recurrence to a better monetary system, it is said, though highly desirable, tends to give a temporary discouragement to accumulation and industry, by depressing the commercial part of the community, and is the effect of a fall of prices: Mr. Malthus supposes that such an effect will be produced by the fall of the price of corn. If the observation made by Hume were well founded, still it would not apply to the present instance, for everything that the manufacturer would have to sell would be as dear as ever: it is only what he would buy that would be cheap, namely corn and labour by which his gains would be increased. I must again observe that a rise in the value of money lowers all things; whereas a fall in the price of corn, only lowers the wages of labour, and therefore raises profits.

If then the prosperity of the commercial classes, will most certainly lead to accumulation of capital, and the encouragement of productive industry; these can by no means be so surely obtained as by a fall in the price of corn.

I cannot agree with Mr. Malthus in his approbation of the

opinion of Adam Smith, 'that no equal quantity of productive labour employed in manufactures, can ever occasion so great a re-production as in agriculture'. I suppose that he must have over-looked the term ever in this passage, otherwise the opinion is more consistent with the doctrine of the Economists, than with those which he has maintained; as he has stated, and I think correctly, that in the first settling of a new country, and in every stage of its improvement, there is a portion of its capital employed on the land for the profits of stock merely, and which yields no rent whatever. Productive labour employed on such land never does in fact afford so great a reproduction, as the same productive labour employed in manufactures.

The difference is not indeed great, and is voluntarily relinquished, on account of the security and respectability which attends the employment of capital on land. In the infancy of society, when no rent is paid, is not the re-production of value in the coarse manu-factures, and in the implements of husbandry with a given capital, at least as great as the value which the same capital would afford if employed on the land?

This opinion indeed is at variance with all the general doctrines of Mr. Malthus, which he has so ably maintained in this as well as in all his other publications. In the *Inquiry*, speaking of what I consider a similar opinion of Adam Smith, he observes, 'I cannot, however, agree with him in thinking that all land which yields food must necessarily yield rent. The land which is successively taken into cultivation, in improving countries may only pay profits and labour. A fair profit on the stock employed, including, of course, the payment of labour, will always be a sufficient inducement to cultivate.' The same motives will also induce some to manufacture goods, and the profits of both in the same stages of society will be nearly the same.

In the course of these observations, I have often had occasion to insist, that rent never falls without the profits of stock rising. If it suits us today to import corn rather than grow it, we are solely influenced by the cheaper price. If we import, the portion of capital last employed on the land, and which yielded no rent, will be withdrawn; rent will fall and profits rise, and another portion of capital employed on the land will come under the same description of only yielding the usual profits of stock.

If corn can be imported cheaper than it can be grown on this rather better land, rent will again fall and profits rise, and another and better description of land will now be cultivated for profits only. In every step of our progress, profits of stock increase and rents fall, and more land is abandoned: besides which, the country saves all the difference between the price at which corn can be grown, and the price at which it can be improved, on the quantity we receive from abroad.

Mr. Malthus has considered, with the greatest ability, the effect of a cheap price of corn on those who contribute to the interest of our enormous debt. I most fully concur in many of his conclusions on this part of the subject. The wealth of England would, I am persuaded, be considerably augmented by a great reduction in the price of corn, but the whole money value of that wealth would be diminished. It would be diminished by the whole difference of the money value of the corn consumed,—it would be augmented by the increased exchangeable value of all those commodities which would be exported in exchange for the corn imported. The latter would, however, be very unequal to the former; therefore the money value of the commodities of England would, undoubtedly, be considerably lowered.

But, though it is true, that the money value of the mass of our commodities would be diminished, it by no means follows, that our annual revenue would fall in the same degree. The advocates for importation ground their opinion of the advantages of it on the conviction that the revenue would not so fall. And, as it is from our revenue that taxes are paid, the burthen might not be really augmented.

Suppose the revenue of a country to fall from ten to nine millions, whilst the value of money altered in the proportion of ten to eight, such country would have a larger neat revenue, after paying a million from the smaller, than it would have after paying it from the larger sum.

That the stockholder would receive more in real value than what he contracted for, in the loans of the late years, is also true; but, as the stockholders themselves contribute very largely to the public burthens, and therefore to the payment of the interest which they receive, no inconsiderable proportion of the taxes would fall on them; and, if we estimate at its true value the additional profits made by the commercial class, they would still be great gainers, notwithstanding their really augmented contributions.

The landlord would be the only sufferer by paying really more, not only without any adequate compensation, but with lowered rents.

It may indeed be urged, on the part of the stockholder, and those who live on fixed incomes, that they have been by far the greatest sufferers by the war. The value of their revenue has been diminished by the rise in the price of corn, and by the depreciation in the value of paper money, whilst, at the same time, the value of their capital has been very much diminished from the lower price of the funds. They have suffered too from the inroads lately made on the sinking fund, and which, it is supposed, will be still further extended,—a measure of the greatest injustice,—in direct violation of solemn contracts; for the sinking fund is as much a part of the contract as the dividend, and, as a source of revenue, utterly at variance with all sound principles. It is to the growth of that fund that we ought to look for the means of carrying on future wars, unless we are prepared to relinquish the funding system altogether. To meddle with the sinking fund, is to obtain a little temporary aid at the sacrifice of a great future advantage. It is reversing the whole system of Mr. Pitt, in the creation of that fund: he proceeded on the conviction, that, for a small present burthen, an immense future advantage would be obtained; and, after witnessing, as we have done, the benefits which have already resulted from his inflexible determination to leave that fund untouched, even when he was pressed by the greatest financial distress, when 3 per cents were so low as 48, we cannot, I think, hesitate in pronouncing, that he would not have countenanced, had he still lived, the measures which have been adopted.

To recur, however, to the subject before me, I shall only further observe, that I shall greatly regret that considerations for any particular class, are allowed to check the progress of the wealth and population of the country. If the interests of the landlord be of sufficient consequence, to determine us not to avail ourselves of all the benefits which would follow from importing corn at a cheap price, they should also influence us in rejecting all improvements in agriculture, and in the implements of husbandry; for it is as certain that corn is rendered cheap, rents are lowered, and the ability of the landlord to pay taxes, is for a time, at least, as much impaired by such improvements, as by the importation of corn. To be consistent then, let us by the same act arrest improvement, and prohibit importation.

References

1. Mr. Malthus considers, that the surplus of produce obtained in consequence of diminished wages, or of improvements in agriculture, to be one of the causes to raise rent. To me it appears that it will only augment profits.

'The accumulation of capital, beyond the means of employing it on land of the greatest natural fertility, and the greatest advantage of situation, must necessarily lower profits; while the tendency of population to increase beyond the means of subsistence must, after a certain time, lower the wages of labour.

'The expense of production will thus be diminished, but the value of the produce, that is, the quantity of labour, and of the other products of labour besides corn which it can command instead of diminishing, will be increased.

'There will be an increasing number of people demanding subsistence, and ready to offer their services in any way in which they can be useful. The exchangeable value of food will therefore be in excess above the cost of production, including in this cost the full profits of the stock employed upon the land, according to the actual rate of profits at the time being. And this excess is rent.'—*An Inquiry into the Nature and Progress of Rent*, page 18.

In page 19, speaking of Poland, one of the causes of rent is again attributed to cheapness of labour. In page 22 it is said that a fall in the wages of labour, or a reduction in the number of labourers necessary to produce a given effect, in consequence of agricultural improvements, will raise rent.

2. It is not meant that strictly the rate of profits on agriculture and manufactures will be the same, but that they will bear some proportion to each other. Adam Smith has explained why profits are somewhat less on some employments of capital than on others, according to their security, cleanliness and respectability, etc. etc.

What the proportion may be, is of no importance to my argument, as I am only desirous of proving that the profits on agricultural capital cannot materially vary, without occasioning a similar variation in the profits on capital, employed on manufactures and commerce.

3. Profits of stock fall because land equally fertile cannot be obtained, and, through the whole progress of society, profits are regulated by the difficulty or facility of procuring food. This is a principle of great importance, and has been almost overlooked in the writings of Political Economists. They appear to think that profits of stock can be raised by commercial causes, independently of the supply of food.

4. In all that I have said concerning the origin and progress of rent, I have briefly repeated and endeavoured to elucidate the principles which Mr. Malthus has so ably laid down, on the same subject, in his *Inquiry into the Nature and Progress of Rent*; a work abounding in original ideas,—which are useful not only as they regard rent, but as connected with the question of taxation; perhaps, the most difficult and intricate of all the subjects on which Political Economy treats.

5. It is scarcely necessary to observe, that the data on which this table is constructed are assumed, and are probably very far from the truth. They were fixed on as tending to illustrate the principle, —which would be the same, whether the first profits were 50 per cent or five,—or whether an additional capital of ten quarters, or, of one hundred, were required to obtain the same produce from the cultivation of new land. In proportion as the capital employed on the land, consisted more of fixed capital, and less of circulating capital, would rent advance, and property fall less rapidly.

6. This would be the effect of a constantly accumulating capital, in a country which refused to import foreign and cheaper corn. But after profits have very much fallen, accumulation will be checked, and capital will be exported to be employed in those countries where food is cheap and profits high. All European colonies have been established with the capital of the mother countries, and have thereby checked accumulation. That part of the population too, which is employed in the foreign carrying trade, is fed with foreign corn. It cannot be doubted that low profits, which are the inevitable effects of a really high price of corn, tend to draw capital abroad;

this consideration ought therefore to be a powerful reason to prevent us from restricting importation.

7. By rent I always mean the remuneration given to the landlord for the use of the original and inherent power of the land. If either the landlord expends capital on his own land, or the capital of a preceding tenant is left upon it at the expiration of his lease, he may obtain what is indeed called a larger rent, but a portion of this is evidently paid for the use of capital. The other portion only is paid for the use of the original power of the land.

8. Excepting, as has been before observed, the real wages of labour should rise, or a worse system of agriculture be practised.

9. The low price of corn, caused by improvements in agriculture, would give a stimulus to population, by increasing profits and encouraging accumulation, which would again raise the price of corn and lower profits. But a larger population could be maintained at the same price of corn, the same profits, and the same rents. Improvements in agriculture may then be said to increase profits, and to lower for a time rents.

10. The causes, which render the acquisition of an additional quantity of corn more difficult are, in progressive countries, in constant operation, whilst marked improvements in agriculture, or in the implements of husbandry are of less frequent occurrence. If these opposite causes acted with equal effect, corn would be subject only to accidental variation of price, arising from bad seasons, from greater or less real wages of labour, or from an alteration in the value of the precious metals, proceeding from their abundance or scarcity.

11. Though the price of all commodities is ultimately regulated by, and is always tending to, the cost of their production, including the general profits of stock, they are all subject, and perhaps corn more than most others, to an accidental price, proceeding from temporary causes.

12. It has been thought that the price of corn regulates the prices of all other things. This appears to me to be a mistake. If the price of corn is affected by the rise or fall of the value of the precious metals themselves, then indeed will the price of commodities be also affected, but they vary, because the value of money varies, not because the value of corn is altered. Commodities, I think, cannot materially rise or fall, whilst money and commodities continue in

the same proportions, or rather whilst the cost of production of both estimated in corn continues the same. In the case of taxation, a part of the price is paid for the liberty of using the commodity, and does not continue its real price.

13. Mr. Malthus has supplied me with a happy illustration—he has correctly compared 'the soil to a great number of machines, all susceptible of continued improvement by the application of capital to them, but yet of very different original qualities and powers'. How, I would ask, can profits rise whilst we are obliged to make use of that machine which has the worst original qualities and powers? We cannot abandon the use of it; for it is the condition on which we obtain the food necessary for our population, and the demand for food is by the supposition not diminished—but who would consent to use it if he could make greater profits elsewhere?

14. Excepting when the extension of commerce enables us to obtain food at really cheaper prices.

15. If by foreign commerce, or the discovery of machinery, the commodities consumed by the labourer should become much cheaper, wages would fall; and this, as we have before observed, would raise the profits of the farmer, and therefore, all other profits.

16. This principle is most ably stated by Mr. Malthus in page 42 of *An Inquiry*, etc.

17. It is this latter opinion which is chiefly insisted upon by Mr. Malthus, in his late publication, *The Grounds of An Opinion*, etc.

18. As London is to be a depot for foreign corn, this store might be very great.

19. If it be true, as Mr. Malthus observes, that in Ireland there are no manufacturers in which capital could be profitably employed, capital would not be withdrawn from the land, and then there would be no loss of agricultural capital. Ireland would, in such case, have the same surplus corn produce, although it would be of less exchangeable value. Her revenue might be diminished; but if she would not, or could not manufacture goods, and would not cultivate the ground, she would have no revenue at all.

20. I by no means agree with Adam Smith, or with Mr. Malthus, respecting the effects of taxation on the necessaries of life. The former can find no term too severe by which to characterize them. Mr. Malthus is more lenient. They both think that such taxes, incalculably more than any other, tend to diminish capital and

production. I do not say that they are the best of taxes, but they do not, I think, subject us to any of the disadvantages of which Adam Smith speaks in foreign trade: nor do they produce effects very different from other taxes. Adam Smith thought that such taxes fell exclusively on the landholder; Mr. Malthus thinks they are divided between the landholder and consumer. It appears to me that they are paid wholly by the consumer.

21. Page 22, *Grounds*, etc.
22. *Grounds*, etc., p. 32.

ABSOLUTE VALUE AND EXCHANGEABLE VALUE

Later Version—Unfinished

Exchangeable Value

By exchangeable value is meant the power which a commodity has of commanding any given quantity of another commodity, without any reference whatever to its absolute value. We should say that an ounce of gold had increased in exchangeable value in relation to cloth if from usually commanding two yards of cloth in the market, it could freely command or exchange for three: and for the same reason we should under the same circumstances say that the exchangeable value of cloth had fallen with respect to gold, as three yards had become necessary to command the same quantity of gold that two yards would command before. Any commodity having value will measure exchangeable value, for exchangeable value and proportional value mean the same thing. By knowing that an ounce of gold will at any particular time exchange for two yards of cloth, ten yards of linen, a hundred weight of sugar, a quarter of wheat, 3 quarters of oats etc. etc. we know the proportional value of all these commodities, and are enabled to say that a yard of cloth is worth 5 yards of linen, and a quarter of wheat 3 times the value of a quarter of oats.

Absolute Value[1]

All measures of length are measures of absolute as well as relative length. Suppose linen and cloth to be liable to contract and expand, by measuring them at different times with a foot rule, which was itself neither liable to contract or expand, we should be able to determine what alteration had taken place in their length. If at one time the cloth measured 200 feet and at another 202, we should say it had increased 1 per cent. If the linen from 100 feet in length increased to 103 we should say it had increased 3 per cent, but we should not say the foot measure had diminished in length because it bore a less proportion to the length of the cloth and linen. The alteration would really be in the cloth and linen and not in the foot measure. In the same manner if we had a perfect measure of value, itself being neither liable to increase or diminish in value, we should by its means be able to ascertain the real as well as the proportional variations in other things and should never refer the variation in the commodity measured to the commodity itself by which it was measured. Thus in the case before stated when an ounce of gold exchanged for two yards of cloth and afterwards exchanged for three, if gold was a perfect measure of value we should not say that gold had increased in value because it would exchange for more cloth but that cloth had fallen in value because it would exchange for less gold. And if gold was liable to all the variations of other commodities, we might, if we knew the laws which constituted a measure of value a perfect one, either fix on some other commodity in which all the conditions of a good measure existed, by which to correct the apparent variations of other things, and thus ascertain whether gold or cloth, or both had varied in real value, or in default of such a commodity we might correct the measure chosen by allowing for the effect of those causes which we had previously ascertained to operate on value.

By many Political Economists it is said that we have an absolute measure of value, not indeed in any one single commodity but in the mass of commodities. If we wanted to ascertain whether in the case just supposed of the cloth and gold the variation had been in the one or in the other, we could immediately ascertain it by comparing them alternately to many other commodities and if the labour required to produce them,—that if a quantity of shrimps required the labour of ten men for one day, a quantity of cloth the labour of ten men for one year, and a quantity of wine required the

that gold preserved the same relation as before with these commodities, then the cloth had varied, but if changed for one and no more we might safely conclude that gold had varied.

of a commodity on the production of which

This measure might be an accurate one on many occasions, but suppose that on such a comparison I found that with respect to a great number gold had altered in value, and with respect to

be precisely 365 times the value of the shrimps for in addition to such value, if profits were 10 pct., 10 pct. must be added on all the advances made for the time they were made before the commodity was brought to market. It would not be true either that the wine would be of only twice the value of the cloth, it would be more for the clothier would be entitled to one years profits only, the wine merchant would be entitled to two. In the second place, if profits fell from 10 pct. to 5 pct., the proportions between the value of wine, of cloth and of shrimps would alter accordingly, although no alteration whatever took place in the quantity of labour necessary to produce these commodities respectively. Now which of these commodities should we chuse for our standard? they would be all unerring, if the quantity of labour employed on production were the sole test of value, and

measure which is not itself invariable. If we have any doubts respecting the uniformity of our measure of length, the foot, for example, we can refer it to a portion of the arc of the meridian, or to the vibrations of the Pendulum under given circumstances and by such means can correct any accidental variations. If we have any doubts respecting our clocks and watches we regulate them by the daily revolution of the earth on its axis, and by similar tests we are enabled to correct our measures of weight and our measures of capacity, but to what standard are we to refer for the correction of our measure of value? It has been said that we are not without a standard in nature to which we may refer for the correction of errors and deviations in our measure of value, in the same way as in the other measures which I have noticed, and that such standard is to be found in the labour of men. The average strength of a thousand or of ten thousand men it is asserted is always nearly the same, why then not make the labour of man the unit or standard measure of value? If we are in possession of any commodity which requires always the same quantity of labour to produce it, that commodity must be of uniform value, and is

Two Writings by David Ricardo

they all vary with respect to each other. If we selected cloth, when profits fell to 5 pc$^{t.}$ shrimps would rise in value, and wine would fall. If we selected wine shrimps would rise very considerably, and cloth would rise in a slight degree; and if we selected shrimps, both wine and cloth would fall considerably, but the wine more than the cloth.

If all commodities were produced by labour alone, without any advances, and were brought to market in one day, then indeed we should possess an uniform measure of value, and any commodity which always required the same quantity of labour to produce it would be as perfect a measure of value, as a foot is a perfect measure of length, or a pound a perfect measure of weight.

Or if all commodities were produced by labour employed upon them for one year, then also would any commodity always requiring the same quantity of labour be a perfect measure.

Or if they were all produced in two years the same would be equally true, but while commodities are produced under the greatest variety of circumstances, as far as regards the time at which they are brought to market, they will not vary only on account of the greater or less quantity of labour necessary to produce them, but also on account of the greater or less proportion of the finished commodity which may be paid to the workman, accordingly as labour is abundant or scarce, or as the necessaries of the workman become more difficult to produce, and which is the only cause of the variation of profits. A commodity produced by labour alone in one day is totally unaffected by a variation in profits, and a commodity produced in one year is less affected by a variation in profits than a commodity produced in two.

It appears then that any commodity always produced by the same quantity of labour, whether employed for a day a month a year or any number of years is a perfect measure of value, if the proportions into which commodities are divided for wages and profits are always alike, but that there can be no perfect measure of the variations in the value of commodities arising from an alteration in these proportions, as the proportions will themselves differ according as the commodity employed for the measure may be produced in a shorter or longer time.

It must then be confessed that there is no such thing in nature as a perfect measure of value, and that all that is left to the Political

Economist is to admit that the great cause of the variation of commodities is the greater or less quantity of labour that may be necessary to produce them, but that there is also another though much less powerful cause of their variation, which arises from the different proportions in which finished commodities may be distributed between master and workman in consequence of either the amended or deteriorated condition of the labourer, or of the greater difficulty or facility of producing the necessaries essential to his subsistence.

But though we cannot have a perfect measure of value is not one of the measures produced by labour better than another, and in chusing amongst measures which are all acknowledged to be imperfect which shall we select[,] one which is produced by labour alone, or one produced by labour employed for a certain period, say a year?

To me it appears most clear that we should chuse a measure produced by labour employed for a certain period, and which always supposes an advance of capital, because $1^{st.}$ it is a perfect measure for all commodities produced under the same circumstances of time as the measure itself—$2^{dly.}$, By far the greatest number of commodities which are the objects of exchange are produced by the union of capital and labour, that is to say of labour employed for a certain time $3^{dly.}$ That a commodity produced by labour employed for a year is a mean between the extremes of commodities produced on one side by labour and advances for much more than a year, and on the other by labour employed for a day only without any advances, and the mean will in most cases give a much less deviation from truth than if either of the extremes were used as a measure. Let us suppose money to be produced in precisely the same time as corn is produced, that would be the measure proposed by me, provided it always required the same uniform quantity of labour to produce it, and if it did not provided an allowance were made for the alteration in the value of the measure itself in consequence of its requiring more or less labour to obtain it. The circumstances of this measure being produced in the same length of time as corn, and most other vegetable food which forms by far the most valuable article of daily consumption, would decide me in giving it a preference.

Mr. Malthus proposes another measure and he supposes a

money to be picked up by the labour of a day on the sea-shore and whatever quantity can be so uniformly picked up is according to him not only the best but a perfect measure [of] value. Thus suppose a man by a day's labour could always pick up as much silver as we call 2/- a day's labour and 2/- would be of equal value and either in Mr. Malthus's judgement would be a perfect measure of value.

Now that it cannot be a perfect measure of value must be evident from the foregoing observations, but it is singular that Mr. Malthus himself after the admissions which he has made for it should claim for it that character. Mr. Malthus acknowledges that if all commodities were produced by the union of capital and labour in the same time that corn is produced[,] that corn always requiring the same quantity of labour or gold produced under the same circumstances as corn would be a perfect measure of value. Mr. Malthus admits then that for a large class of commodities the measure proposed by me is a perfect one, and that it would be a perfect one for all if the case were as I have just supposed it. Now let me suppose that corn, cloth, gold and various other commodities to be produced in the same time, and that gold is the measure and always produced with the same quantity of labour. Let me also suppose that labour becomes scarce and is universally paid by a larger proportion of the finished commodity, will corn, or cloth rise in price? Will it exchange for more gold the general measure? Mr. Malthus has admitted and will admit that it would not, because this rise of wages will affect all equally, and will therefore leave them in the same relative situation to each other. If the labourers in agriculture receive $\frac{3}{4}$ of the produce, in lieu of one half, as wages, the labourers in the gold mines, and in the clothiers manufactory will do the same, and consequently the prices of these commodities, their value in this (under these circumstances acknowledged) perfect measure will remain unaltered. Now, suppose Mr. Malthus's money obtained by the labour of a day to be the measure of value, will corn and cloth under the former supposition of a larger proportion of the whole produce being paid to the workman, remain of the same value? certainly not: every quarter of corn will command less labour, less of Mr. Malthus' money and therefore will be of less value. Here then are two measures both perfect according to Mr. Malthus in one of which the same commodities will remain stationary that vary in the other.

If I had no argument to advance against the expediency of adopting Mr. Malthus's proposed measure, this is I think conclusive against the claim which he sets up for its universal accuracy and perfection, but I have many reasons to urge against its adoption on account of its inexpediency.

Let me suppose that some great improvement was discovered in agriculture by means of which we might without any additional labour on the land produce 50 pc^t more of corn. According to my mode of estimating value, without any regard to what was paid to the workman corn would fail in the proportion of 150 to 100. According to Mr. Malthus's mode of estimating the value of corn, it would not depend at all upon the difficulty or facility of producing it, but solely on the quantity paid to the labourer. Altho' you could produce 50 pc^t or 100 pc^t more with the same labour he would say it was of the same value if the labourer received no more than before—according to him commodities are not valuable in proportion to the difficulty or facility of producing them, but their value depends wholly, not on the proportion, but on the actual quantity paid to the labourer. A man can buy in our present money a loaf and a half of bread for the same money that he could before buy only a loaf: he can do so because the facility of producing it is increased 50 pc^t and yet Mr. Malthus would constrain us to say that corn had not fallen in value, but that money had risen in value if the labourer received the same quantity of corn.

An epidemic disorder prevails in a country to so great a degree as to sweep off a very large portion of the people and in consequence all the employers of labour are obliged to give a much larger proportion of their finished commodities to their labourers, this in my estimate of value would have no effect whatever on the price of goods, but it would have a great effect on the price of labour. Wages I should say were high and specifically because labour was scarce as compared with capital, not so Mr. Malthus, he would say that labour remained precisely of the same value, and that all commodities without exception which were the produce of labour and capital had undergone a considerable reduction of value.

A vast number of people come into this country from Ireland and by their competition sink the price of labour. Mr. Malthus assures us that labour has not altered in value, but that all commodities, in the production of which no new difficulty has occurred, have very considerably increased in value.

I know and am ready to confess that however these expressions might be contrary to general usage, if Mr. Malthus had shewn that the alteration he proposed rested on a sound principle, we ought, at least amongst Political Economists, to have adopted them, but I contend that his selection rests on no sound principle whatever,— that it is an arbitrary choice, and that it has no foundation in reason and truth. My measure says Mr. Malthus is an invariable one because it will measure both wages and profits. 'I can see no impropriety', he says, 'in saying with Adam Smith and myself that labour will measure not only that part of the whole value of the commodity which resolves itself into labour but also that which resolves itself into profits.'[2] Nor no body else if the object be to determine the proportions into which the whole value is divided between the capitalist and the labourer, but what proof does this afford of its being an invariable measure of value? Would not gold, silver, iron, lead, cloth, corn—all confessedly variable measures— equally effect the proposed object? The question is about an invariable measure of value, and the proof of the invariability of the proposed measure is that it will measure profits as well as labour, that is to say that it will do what every other measure without exception variable or invariable will equally accomplish.[3]

But the conditions of the supply of every commodity says Mr. Malthus are that it should command more labour than it cost, and therefore labour is a particularly appropriate measure. That is saying in other words that wherever advances are made, if those advances only are returned, and nothing remains for profit, the commodity will not be produced. This is a proposition which no one denies but it does not afford the least proof of the invariability of the value of labour, for if a man value his advances, in labour, and his returns in the same medium, his profits will be increased if labour during the interval that he is obtaining the returns become very abundant, they will be reduced to little or nothing if labour become scarce. But so also they would be if he made these estimates in money. If labour rose in money he would realise less

money for profits when he was obliged to give a great deal of
money to his labourers, he would realize more money for profits if
in consequence of the fall of the price of labour he had to pay his
labourers a small quantity of money. Mr. Malthus appears to me
wholly to fail in his proof of labour being invariable in value.

Mr. MCulloch has a different theory—he does not he says[4]
pretend to establish any general invariable measure of value, but
all he aims at is to lay down the rule by which the relative value of
commodities may be determined and this he says depends on the
quantity of labour worked up in them. If one commodity is twice
the value of another, it is because it has twice the quantity of labour
employed on it. It is objected to Mr. MCulloch that this does
not appear to be the fact, that an oak tree worth £100 has not
had perhaps from the first moment it was planted as much labour
employed on it as would cost 5 shillings while another commodity
of the value of £100 had really had 100 pounds worth of labour bestowed on it. Mr. MCulloch answers that he estimates the labour
in a commodity by the capital which has actually been devoted
to its production, and if you again object that only 5/- worth of
capital has been bestowed on the tree he denies this and says 5/-
employed for a day will when profits are 10 pc$^{t.}$ be equivalent to
5/6 in a year, that after the 1$^{st.}$ year, and for the second year 5/6 is
employed as capital which at the end of the 2$^{d.}$ year becomes a
capital of 6/0½ and so from year to year because you forbear
using any part of the capital it becomes in the course of time worth
£100, in the same manner as if you employed 5/- for one day on
the land, in a year it would be worth 5/6. This 5/6 will employ
more labour and will at the end of another year produce 6/0½ and
so on from year to year till it amount to £100. That in fact there
is not so much actual labour bestowed on the tree as on the corn
which may sell for £100 but that equal capitals have been actually
expended on them if you make due allowance for the forbear-
ance of the owner of the 5/- expended on the tree in not appro-
priating to himself any part of the accumulations which the tree
made from year to yea.. If you suppose the growing tree brought to
market every year the first year it will be worth 5/6 the second
6/0½ and so on; that in fact these successive purchasers actually
advance such a sum of capital to become possessed of the tree, till
at last £100 is advanced. Mr. MCulloch asks what are these

advances but capital, what is capital but labour: how then can it be denied that equal quantities of labour yield equal values. If you ask Mr. MCulloch whether the labour of 52 men for one week be not the same quantity of labour as the labour of one man for 52 weeks, he will answer, no, it is not the same, for after each week a man who receives the profit on his work has an increased capital with which to work the second week and so on from week to week; the second man who employs his capital for 52 weeks without receiving any profit during the interval is equally entitled to these successive accumulations, and therefore his capital is to be estimated by the same rule as the man's capital who realises an increased capital every week, by adding to the original capital the further capital which his profits enable him to cultivate. The only doubt one can feel on this subject is the accuracy of the language used by Mr. MCulloch—it might be right to say that commodities were valuable in relation to each other according to their cost of production, or according to the quantity of capital employed on them for equal times, but it does not appear correct to say that their relative value depended on the quantity of capital worked up in them [*The MS breaks off here*]

References

1. In an earlier draft, this section opened as follows: 'But although in the case just supposed we should know the relative value of these commodities we should have no means of knowing their absolute value. If an ounce of gold, from commanding two yards of cloth, came to command 3 yards of cloth, it would alter in relative or exchangeable value to cloth, but we should be ignorant whether gold had risen in absolute value or cloth had fallen in absolute value. Suppose lead to be a measure of absolute value, and that when an ounce of gold exchanged for two yards of cloth it was of the same value as 2 cwt. of lead, and that when it was worth 3 yards of cloth it was worth also 3 cwt. of lead, then cloth would not have varied in absolute value, but gold would have risen 50 pc$^{t.}$ If, on the contrary, the ounce of gold continued of the same value as 2 cwt. of lead, then, when it exchanged for 3 yards of cloth, cloth would have risen 50

pc^{t.} in absolute value and gold would not have varied. The question is, can we obtain such a measure of absolute value and what are the criteria by which we are to satisfy ourselves that we have obtained? Into that question we now propose to enter.

'No one can doubt that it would be a great desideratum in political Ec. to have such a measure of absolute value in order to enable us to know, when commodities altered in exchangeable value, in which the alteration in value had taken place.' Here the draft broke off and started again with the paragraph 'All measures of length'.

2. Malthus's letter of 25 August 1823.
3. See Ricardo's letter to Malthus, 31 August 1823.
4. Cf. McCulloch's letter of 24 August 1823.

Index

Sub-entries are in the order in which they appear throughout the book, and not in alphabetical order.

agriculture, and surplus in Physiocracy 11–12, 13; and rate of profit in Ricardo 62–9, 79–80, 153–80; *see also*, rent
Anderson 63
avances foncières 18, 19
avances primitives 18, 19

bon prix 20, 21, 22
bourgeois economic thought 1 ff.; original concepts of 5; its reaction to its 'crisis' 5
bourgeoisie, properly recognized for the first time in Smith's work 58; *see also*, conflict, class opposition

Cannan 31, 59, 136
capital, in neo-classical thought 3; as 'universal value' 6; and value in Marx 7, in Physiocracy 11–12; and surplus in Physiocracy 22; and surplus in Smith 37–8; accumulation of and rate of profit in Smith 49; supply of and level of economic activity in Smith 51; and labour power in value theory 71; and Ricardo's embodied labour value theory 74–7; and abstract labour in Marx 104–5; distinction in Marx between money and capital 105; opposed to labour in Marx 106; and social exchange in Marx 107–8
capitalistic organization, and its influence on Smith's analysis 46; Ricardo's fully operational concept of 61; profit rate the most important factor in 62; and Ricardo in Parliament 81; and divergence between social product and consumption 90; co-operation the fundamental form of capitalist society 110; competition the essential feature of 100; capital planning inconsistent with, according to Marx 111

capitalist, the superior bargaining position of 'masters' in Smith 47–8

cheapness or plenty, *see* Smith's 'Glasgow Lectures' 137–52

classes, in neo-classical thought 2, 'ranks' of society in Smith, 38, 136; Physiocratic definition of 15; *see also* Quesnay's 'Reply to M.H.' 115 ff.

conflict, class opposition, between landowners and the bourgeoisie in Ricardo 81; between landowners and all other classes in Ricardo 160–1, 175; possibility of between bourgeoisie and proletariat in Ricardo 81–5; in relation to overproduction crises 89; Labour opposed to capital in Marx 106

consumption, unbalanced under capitalism 3

consumers' sovereignty 4

crises: the 1929 economic crisis 1, 2; Marx's theory of 6–7, 91–2; the debate between Ricardo and Malthus on overproduction crises 85–91; 'crisis state' of bourgeois economic thought 1

development, *see also*, growth, accumulation; *also* surplus; international disequilibria of 2–3; free trade possibly harmful to 54

distribution, in neo-classical theory 2, 4; changing pattern of in neo-capitalist society 8; interdependence of value and distribution theory 39; central role of in Ricardo's definition of economic science 61

division of labour, in Smith 32–3, 139–46

Dupont de Nemours 115

exchange, *see also*, value, price; and the Physiocrats 10; and surplus in Physiocracy 13, 18; propensity to exchange in Smith 33–4, 143–5; relationship between social product and labour commanded 44; effective exchange ratio means cost price to Marx 94 n; as the social basis of mercantilism in Marx 100; exchange value as general product or money in Marx 100–1; exchange becomes social only with capital in Marx 107–8; as something alien to the individual in Marx 101–2; the alienating nature of in Marx 108; exchange, commerce and production in Quesnay 126

free trade, *see laissez faire*

growth, accumulation, *see also*, surplus; effect of on employment in Smith 45–6; of capital and rate of profit in Smith 49; limit to in Ricardo 157–60; effect of on income distribution in Ricardo 62–9, 157–60

harmony, *see also* natural order; in marginal theory 2

Hobbes 25–6

Hume 28–9

Hutcheson 29

infant industry. Smith's rejection of import restriction to aid domestic industry 51–2; Smith's arguments inconclusive 53–4.

impôt unique 20

'Industrial Reserve Army' 48

interest, and rate of profit in Smith 49

invisible hand 51

Kant 28

laissez faire, laissez passer, free
trade, and the Physiocrats 20,
130, 131, 134; Smith's espousal
of, 51–3; Ricardo on 81, 154,
164–80; Malthus' position on
criticised by Ricardo 169–80
labour, becomes 'general labour'
only through exchange 110
labour, 'abstract labour', 'mere
labour'. Distinction between
abstract labour and useful
labour in Marx 99; an apparent
ambiguity in Marx's conceptual
presentation of 99; and Marx's
theoretic schema as compared
with Smith's 100; as alien to
the individual 103–4; the
opposite of concrete, useful and
determinate labour 103–4; its
connection with capital 104–5;
mere labour equivalent to
abstract labour in Marx, 105;
mere labour independent of its
product as objectified labour
106; defined with respect to
exchange 109
labour commanded, as measure of
value in Smith 39–43; as
growth criterion for Smith
41–2, 43; Ricardo's rejection of
71; and over-production crises
in Malthus's thought 86–91
labour, estranged or propertyless,
in Marx 106
labour embodied, as measure of
value in Smith 39–42; as
determinator of exchange ratio
in Ricardo 69–71; Ricardo's
use of in analysis of profit rate
74; Ricardo's difficulties with
labour embodied value theory
74–7, and Ricardo's 'invariable
measure of value' 77; Ricardo's
adoption of as decisive element
in value determination 79; and

over-production crises 86–91;
its two-fold character the pivot
of political economy for Marx
99
labour, immediately social, direct
living labour. Discussed by
Marx with reference to pre-
capitalist or future society 102–3
land, *see* agriculture *and* rent
Locke 26–8

Malthus 63, 66; his debate with
Ricardo on over-production
crises 88–91; Ricardo's
acknowledgement of his rent
theory 153–4; Ricardo's
comments on his 'Observations
on the Corn Laws' 169–90;
Mandeville 29, 30
marginalism 5
Marx, Marxist thought, *see* Ch. 5;
the importance to him of the
two-fold character of labour
embodied 99; Marx's treatment
of exchange contrasted with
Smith's 99–104; abstract and
social labour 103–104; Abstract
labour and capital 104–7;
ambiguity of Marx's definition
of abstract labour (*i.e.* deduced
from exchange rather than
capital) shown to be apparent
only 107–9; private labour,
abstract labour, and capitalistic
organisation 109–11
McCulloch, his value theory
criticised by Ricardo 189–90
mercantile, or merchant economy,
in Physiocratic thought 10; in
Smith's thought 36, 61;
'Mercantilist relics' disappear in
Ricardo's thought 61; *but see
also* 82
Mill 66
Mirabeau 14, 23; and Smith 35
miserliness, or niggardliness, of
nature 26

natural order, and state of nature, in Physiocracy 9–10, 20; in Smith 34; *see also* Hobbes, Locke, Hume
natural wants of mankind, in Smith's 'Lectures' 137–9
net product, *see* surplus

overproduction, *see* crises

Physiocrats, *see* Ch. 2; their general approach and the society of their time 9–12; their analysis of net product or surplus 12–15; the mechanism of the *Tableau Economique* 15–17; the significance of rent in the *Tableau* 17–19; their policy recommendations 19–20; the *Tableau* as a description of the *ordre naturel* 20–1; contradictions and difficulties within the Physiocratic schema, 21–2; their influence on Smith 35; *see also* Quesnay
population, and the wage level in Smith 45, 48
price, *see also* value; natural price and market price in Smith's *Lectures* 31–2, 147–52; and scarcity and abundance in Quesnay 119
productivity, and division of labour in Smith 33, 38, 139–46; and capitalism in Smith 38; Smith's treatment of 36–9
profit, Physiocratic treatment of 14–15; ordinary or average rate of in Smith 41, 47, 49; and amount of capital advanced in Smith 37; and interest rate in Smith 49; and accumulation of capital 49; the problem of rate of profit the centre of Ricardo's analysis 62; Ricardo's early analysis of 62–6; general rate determined by agricultural rate

in Ricardo 64, 79–80, 155–6, 163–4; problems arising through its influence on prices in Ricardo 64–6, 79–80; possibility of analysis in terms of a material (corn) rate in Ricardo 79–80; Ricardo's analysis of in terms of labour embodied 74; existence of causing non-equality between *cost prices* and *values* 77; the origin of, left unanswered by Ricardian value theory 91; can only be raised by a fall in the value of food in Ricardo's thought 162
Proudhon 107

Quesnay, on productive and sterile classes 116–26; on the role and functions of the State, 126–35; and Newtonian theory 9 n; and Smith 35; *see also* Ch. 2

rent, and consumption in Physiocracy 18; its dependence on market price in Physiocracy 119–20; 'ordinary or average rate' of in Smith 41, 47; natural rate a maximum rate in Smith 49–50; differential rent in Smith 50; as the effect of monopoly in Smith 49; absolute rent 50; and 'powers of nature' 50; Physiocratic residuum in Smith's theory of 59 n6, 50; Ricardo's early analysis of 62–6, 154–80; rent analysed in terms of a corn model 68, 154–80
Ricardo, *see* Ch. 4 and 153–91; the area and nature of his economic analysis 61–2; his analysis of profit and rent in the *Essay* 62–6, 153–80; how his profit theory could be recast in

purely physical terms 66–9; his
adoption of the labour embodied
approach to value theory 69–71;
his value theory compared
with Smith's 71–4; Ricardo
objections to labour embodied
value theory 74–7; his search
for an 'invariable measure of
value' 77–9, 180–91; and his
thesis that agricultural profit rate
determines general profit
rate, 79–80; the relevance of
his profit theory to class conflict
81; net and gross revenue,
the introduction of machinery,
and class conflict 81–5; Ricardo
and Malthus on overproduction
crises 85–91; comments on the
Ricardo/Malthus controversy
90–2; Ricardo's theory gave
rise to two separate
developments 5; and Smith's
rent theory 50; his trade theory
compared with Smith's 53; his
presupposition of free
competition noted by Marx
111; and Malthus on rent
theory 50, 153–4; his criticism
of Malthus's value theory 185–9;
his criticism of McCulloch's
value theory 189–90

Say 92 n
Self-Interest, its social role 29;
and social utility in Smith
30–1; private vices, public
virtue 30; and society's welfare
in Smith 51
Sismondi 92 n
Smith, *see* Ch. 3; his moral
philosophy 25–31; the economic
analysis of the Lectures 31–4,
136–52; the influence of
Physiocracy 35; His analysis of
productivity and net product
35–9; his value theory 39–42;
his growth theory 43–47, and

the 'natural levels' of wages
profit and rent 47–50; and the
advantages of economic
freedom 51–4; on the role and
functions of the State 54–8; his
real significance 58; Ricardo's
comments on his distribution
theory 92 n.; his value theory
compared with Ricardo's 71–4;
see also the 'Glasgow Lectures'
on the natural wants of
mankind, the division of labour,
and the price of commodities
135–52
social product, division of in
neo-classical thought 2; and
utility 2; connection with
labour commanded 44;
magnitude of *net* product
emphasised by Ricardo 82–3;
gross and net product,
machinery, and employment in
Ricardo's thought 81–4; its
divergence from consumption
under capitalism 91
state intervention, in neo-classical
thought 3–4; bourgeois policy
of 4–5; and Hobbes' 'selfish
system' 25–6; for maintenance
of natural order in Locke 26;
the objects of political economy
in Smith 46; role and functions
of the State in Smith 54–8;
see also Quesnay's 'General
Maxims' 126–39
Stuart 92 n.
surplus, net product, in
Physiocracy 12, 13, 36; and
Tableau Economique 15, 18;
and growth in Physiocracy 19;
and capital in Physiocracy 22;
and division of labour in
Smith 33; rent and profit
components of in Smith 37–9;
and Smith's value theory 41,
43; Marx's labour surplus 42;
and accumulation and

productive labour in Smith
43–4; and accumulation in
feudal society 46; Marx's
theory as applied to Smith's
labour commanded 73; and
employment in Ricardo 81–5
88–90

Tableau Economique, see Ch. 2;
also Quesnay's 'Reply to M.H.
. . .' 116–26
taxation, *see also impôt unique*;
Smith's four principles of 56;
tax sources in Smith 56; tax on
profit, rent, wages, and
'indifferent taxes' in Smith 56–7
trade restriction, two situations
where justified by Smith 52;
two situations where Smith
thought justification possible
52–3; *see also laissez faire.*
Turgot 92 n

utility, 1

value, *see also* exchange, price;
and Marx's concept of capitalist
society 6; value theory and
theory of crises in Marx 7;
contradiction between value and
value in exchange 7; and capital
in Marx 7; no Physiocratic
theory of 12, 21–2; and
distribution theory 39; labour

commanded and labour
embodied value approaches in
Smith 39–42, 70; Marx's
rigorous treatment of
compared with Smith and
Ricardo 44; Ricardo's theory
of based on Smith's 69;
exchange ratio dependent on
labour embodied in Ricardo
69–71; Marx's ideas necessary
for evaluation of Smith's and
Ricardo's theory of 71–2;
difficulties encountered by
Ricardo in the labour embodied
approach 71–7; Ricardo's
search for 'invariable measure'
of 77–9; Ricardo's absolute
value the same as his labour
value 79; interdependence of
profit and value in Ricardo's
analysis 79–80; and
overproduction crises in
Malthus and Ricardo 85–91; in
Marxist analysis 91–2; *see also*
Ricardo's 'Absolute Value and
Exchangeable Value' 180–91

wages, and rate of accumulation in
Smith 45; and population
growth in Smith 45; natural
rate of in Smith 31–2, 35, 36–7;
natural rate a minimum rate in
Smith 47; natural price of
labour in Ricardo 79